Images in this Book

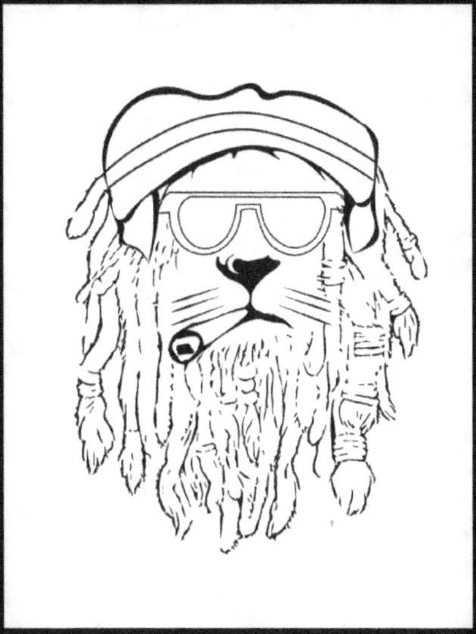

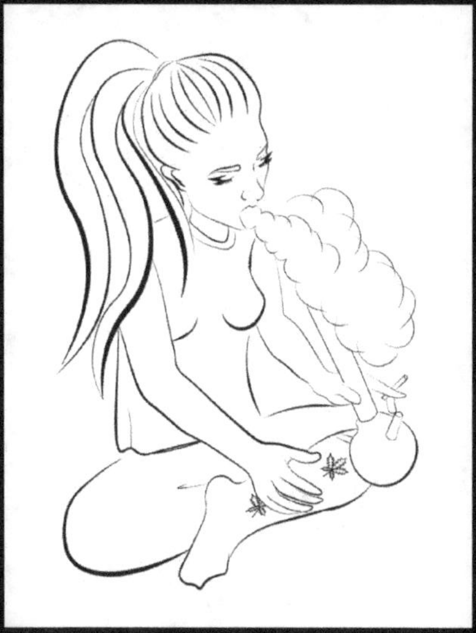

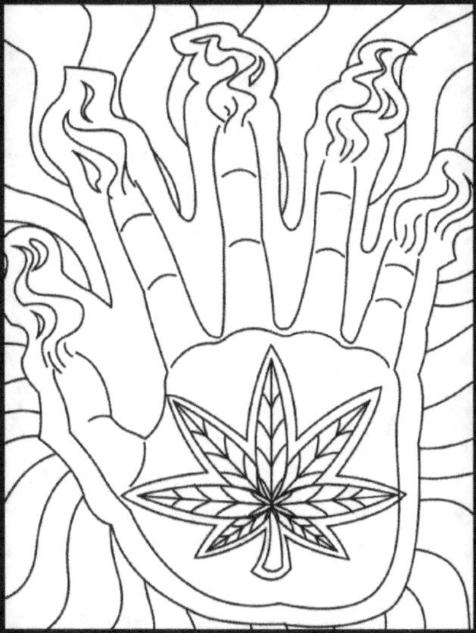

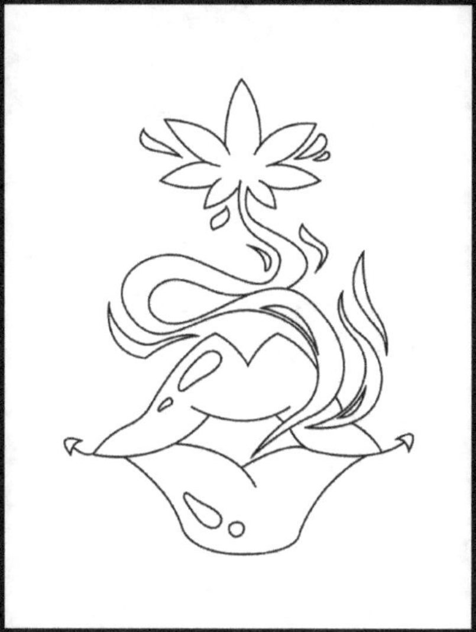

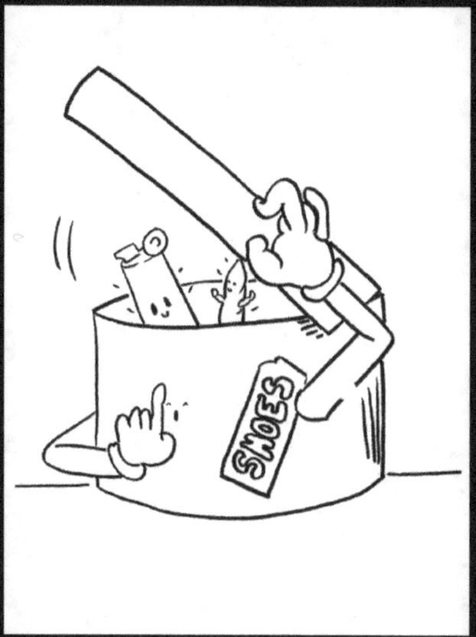

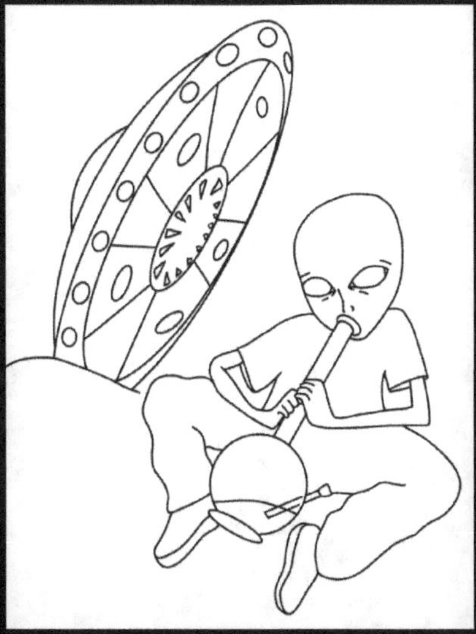

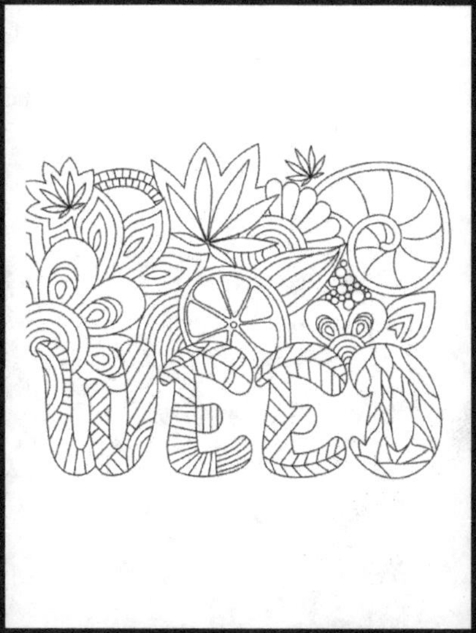

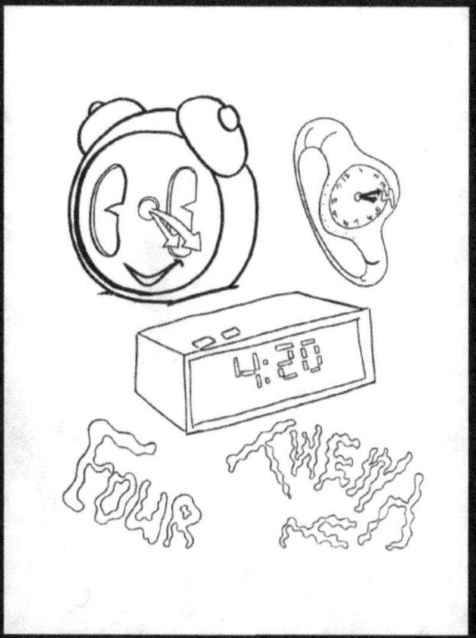

and much more!

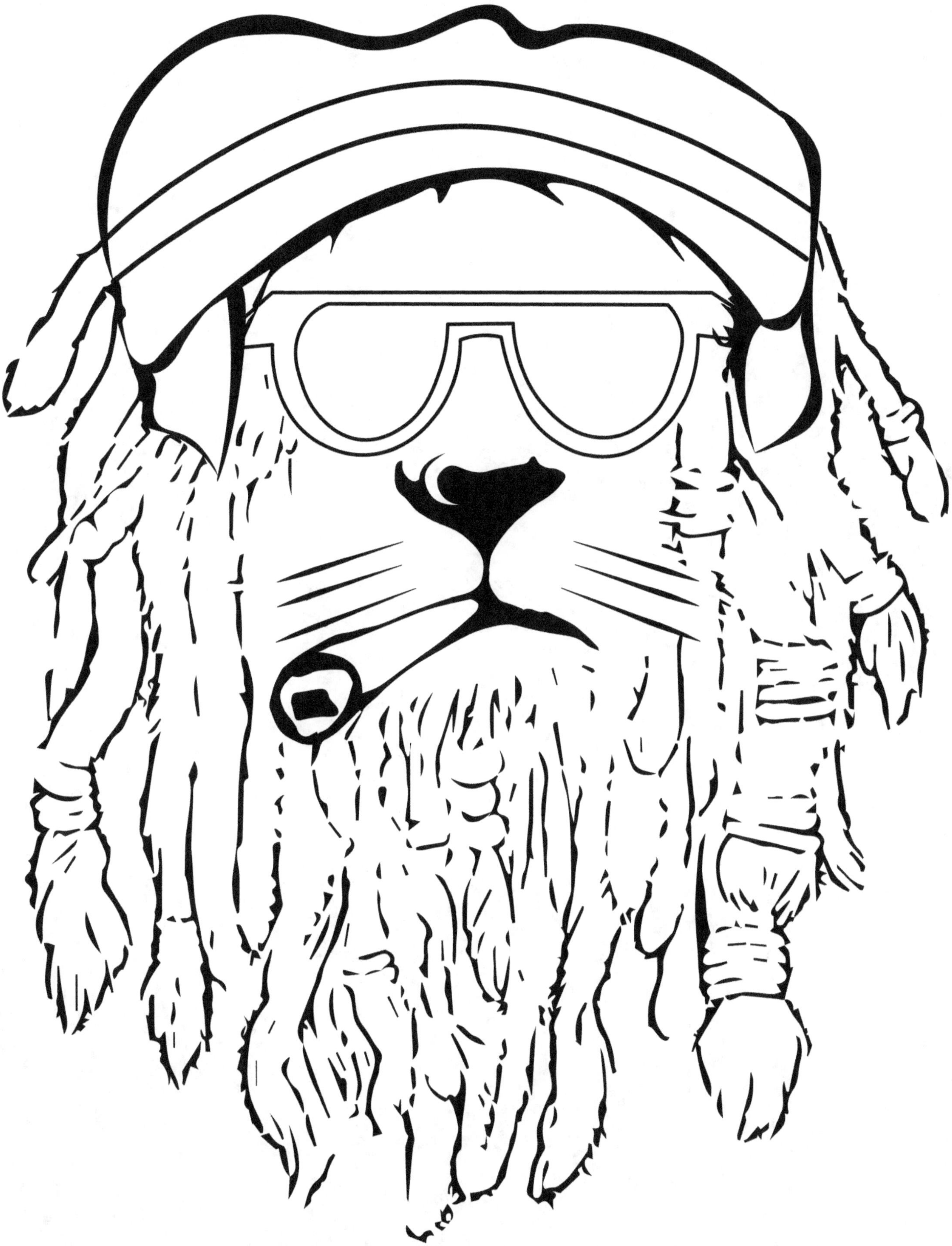

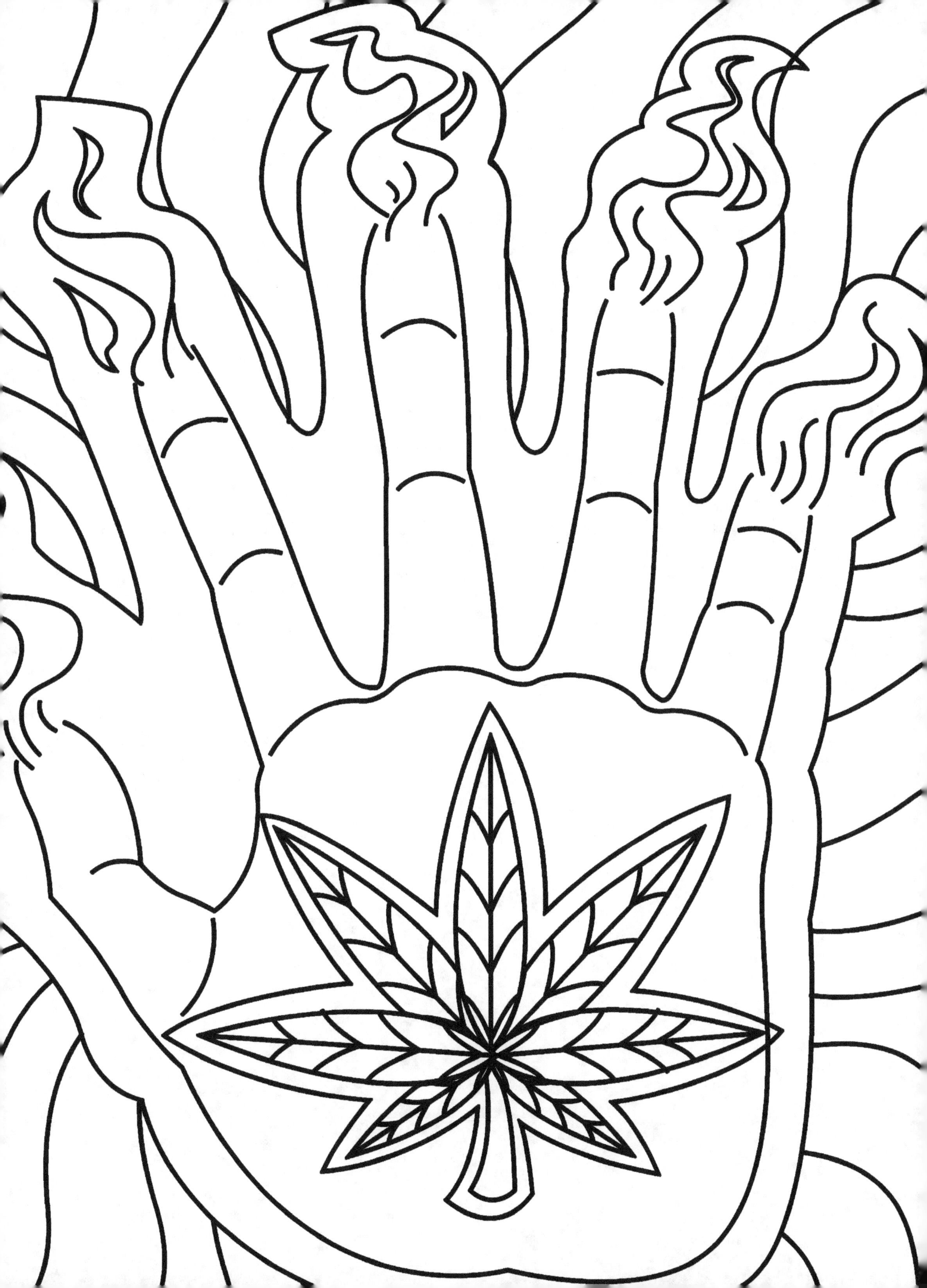

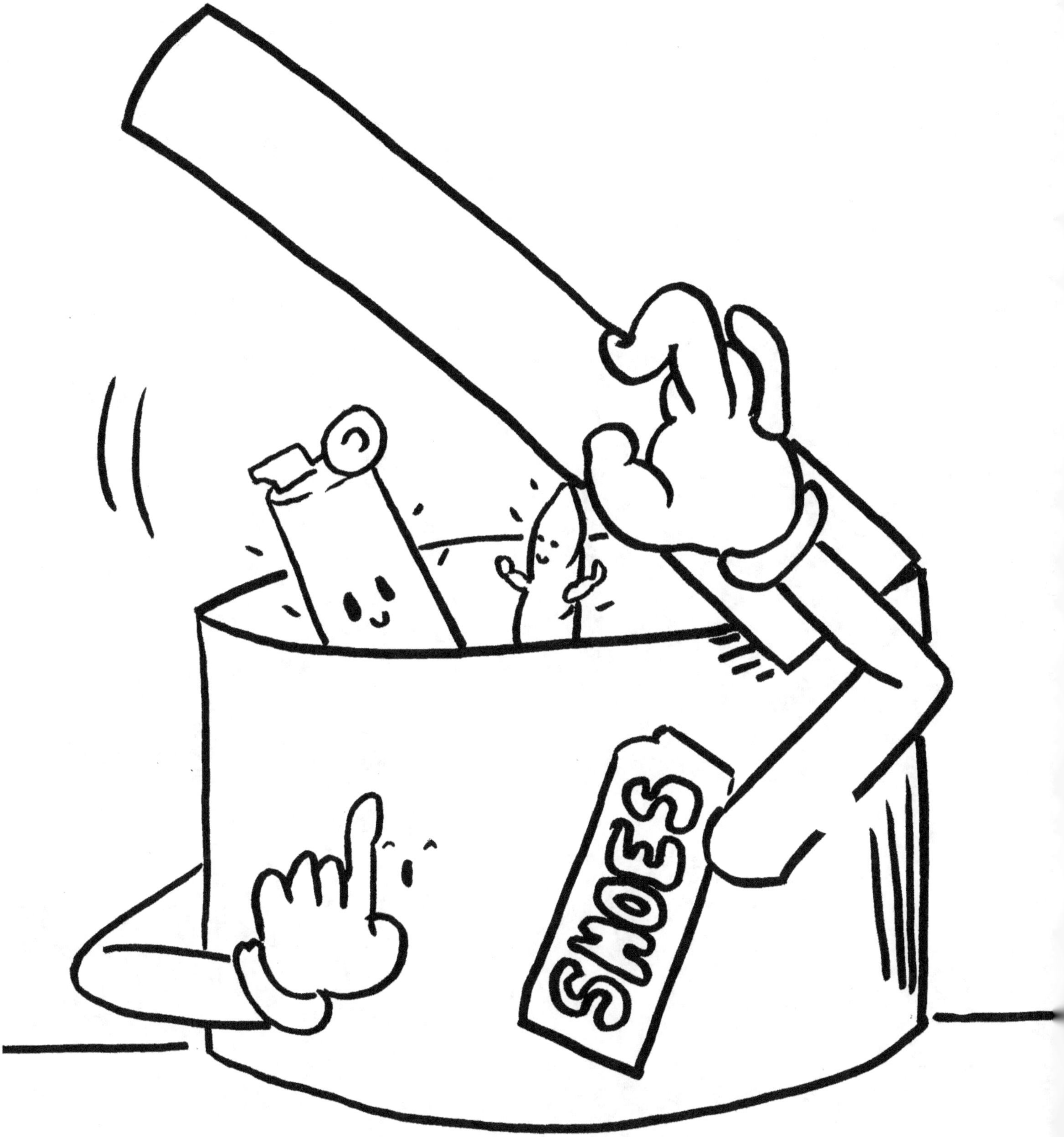
SHOES

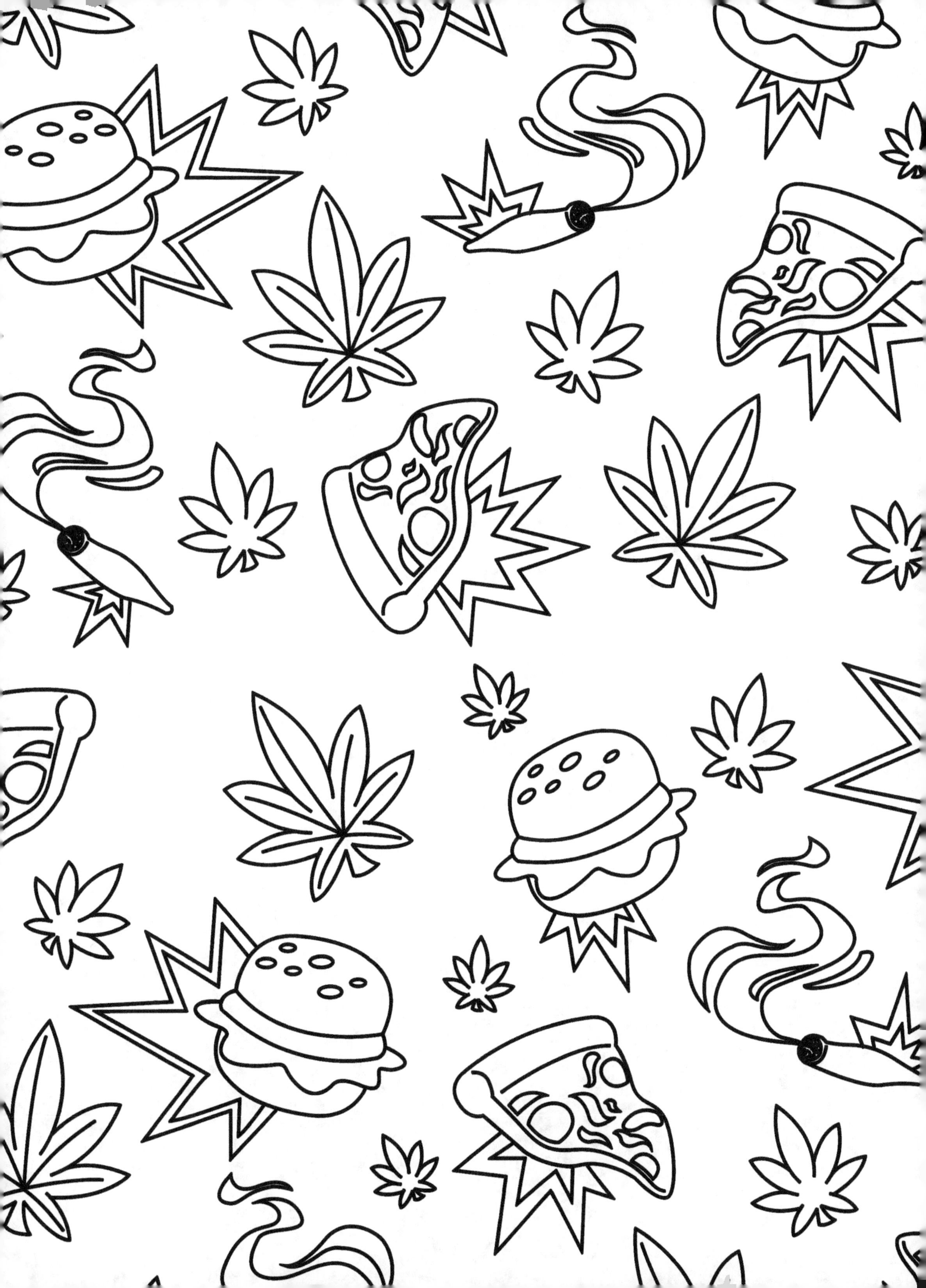

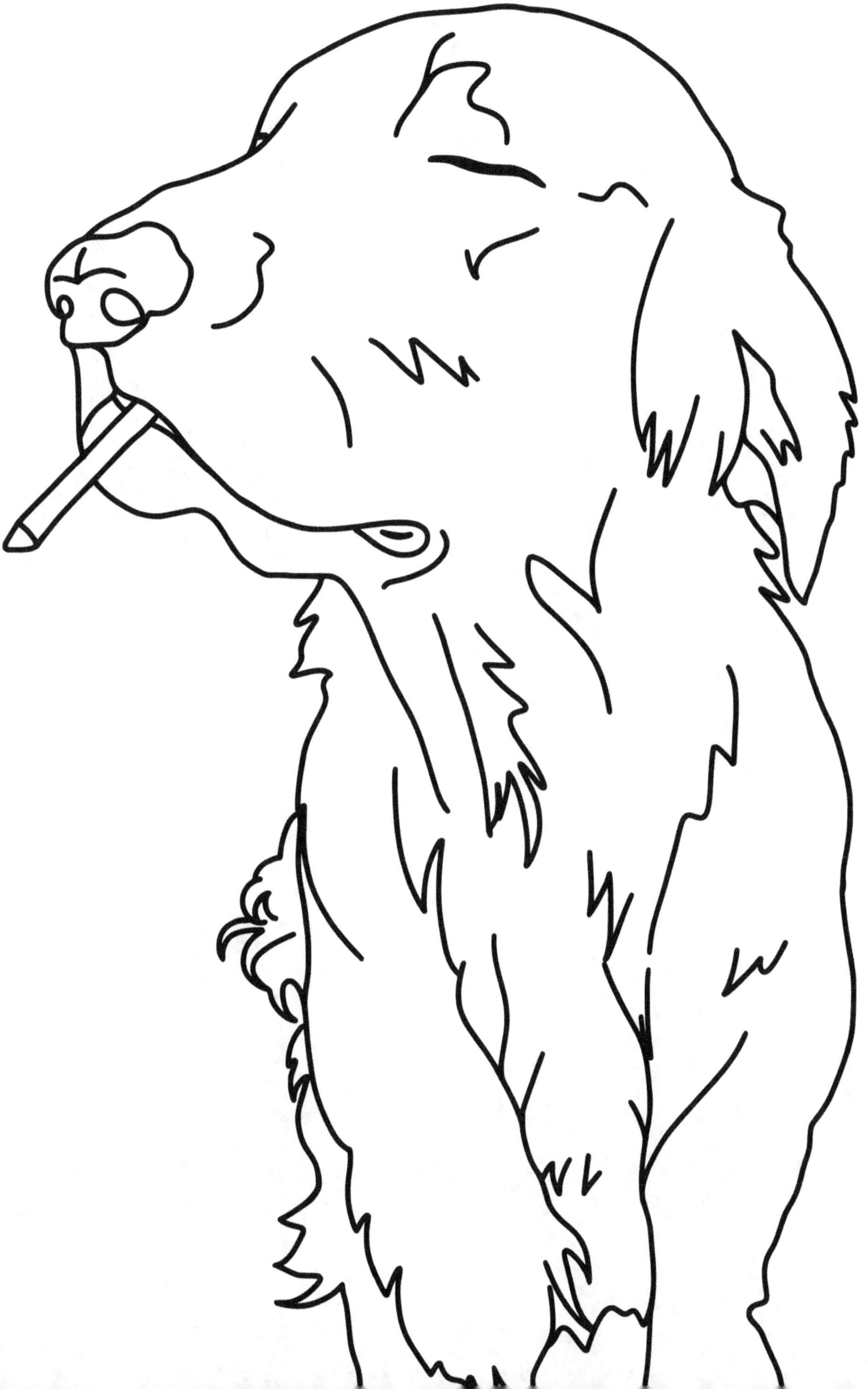

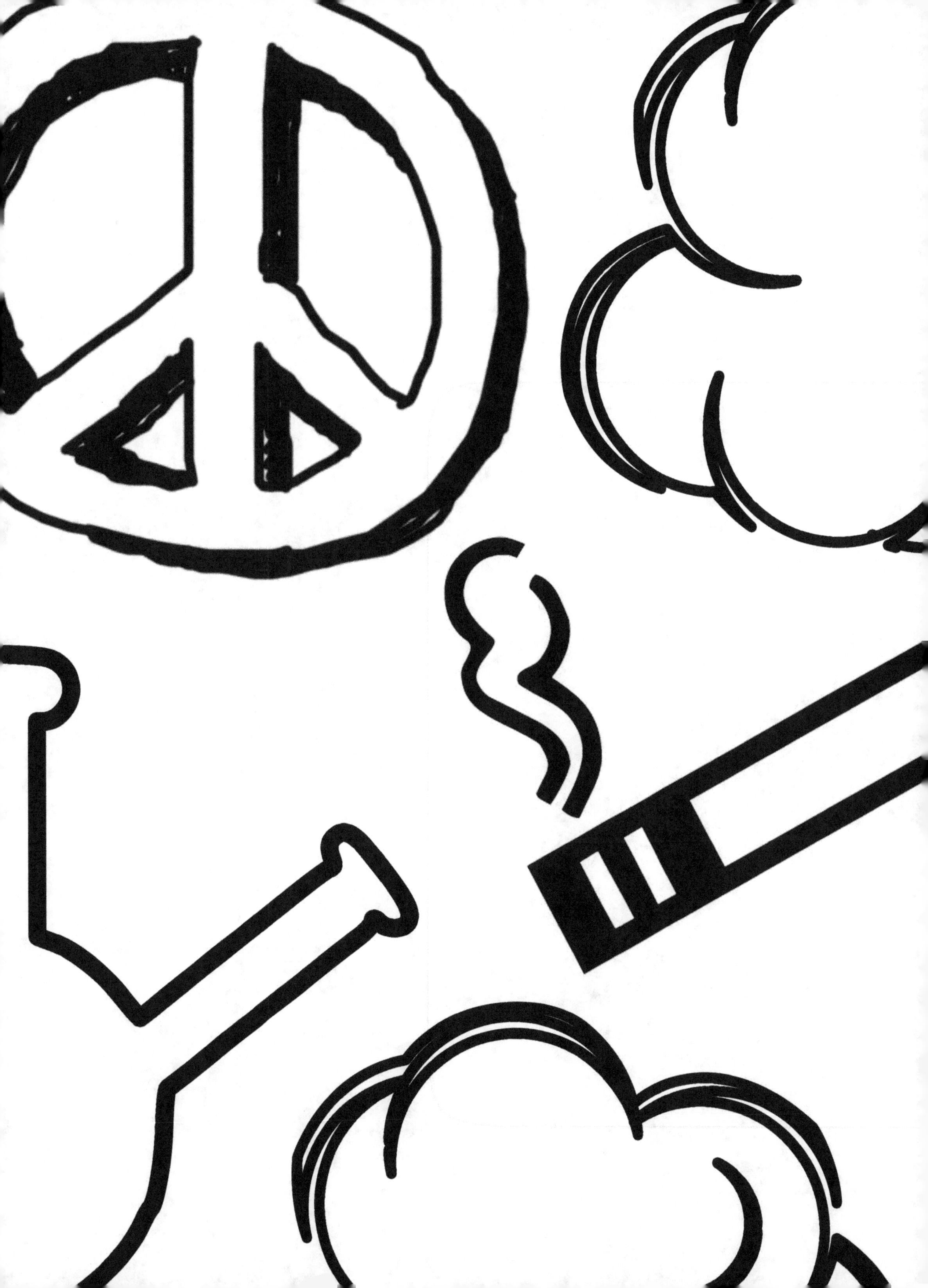

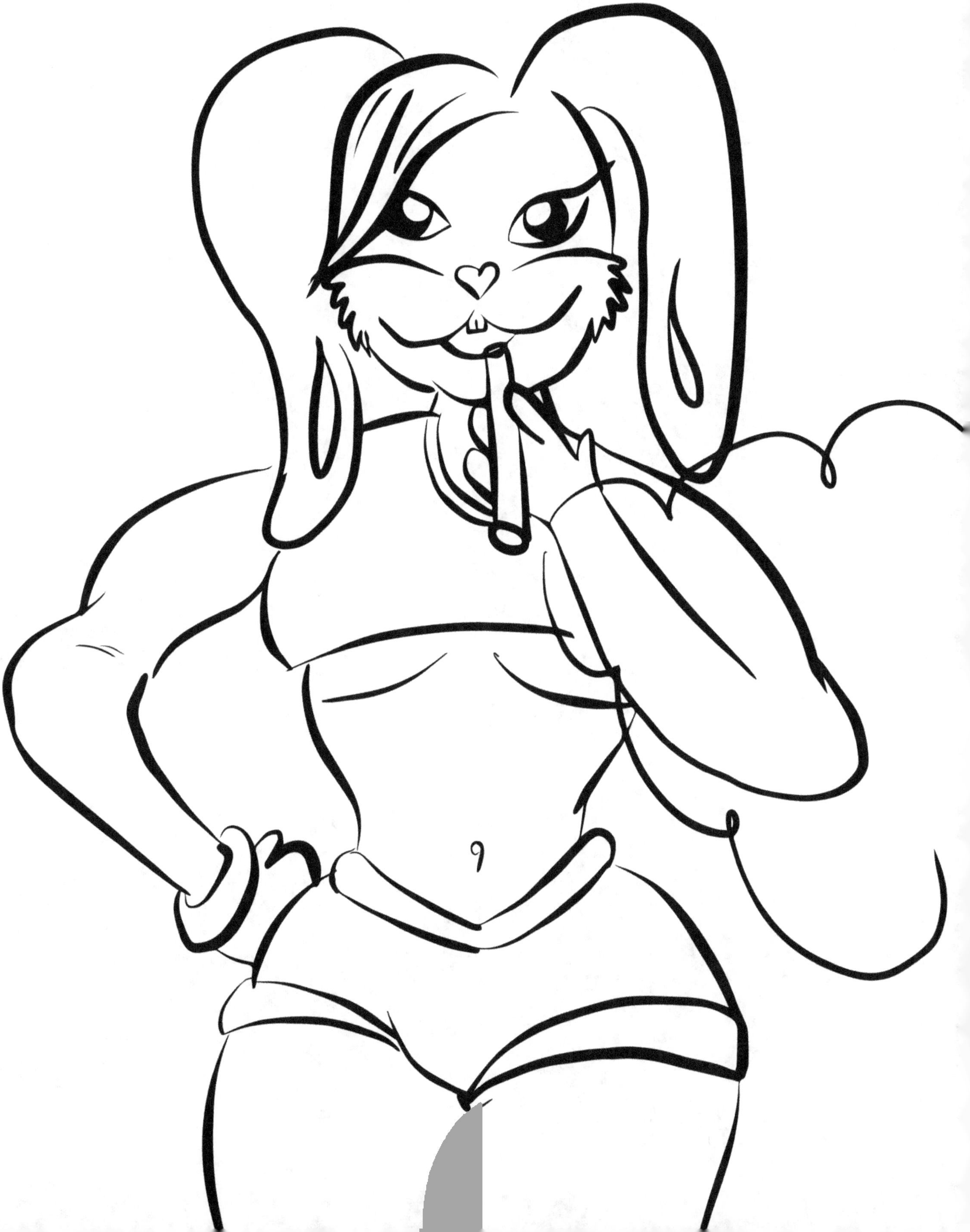

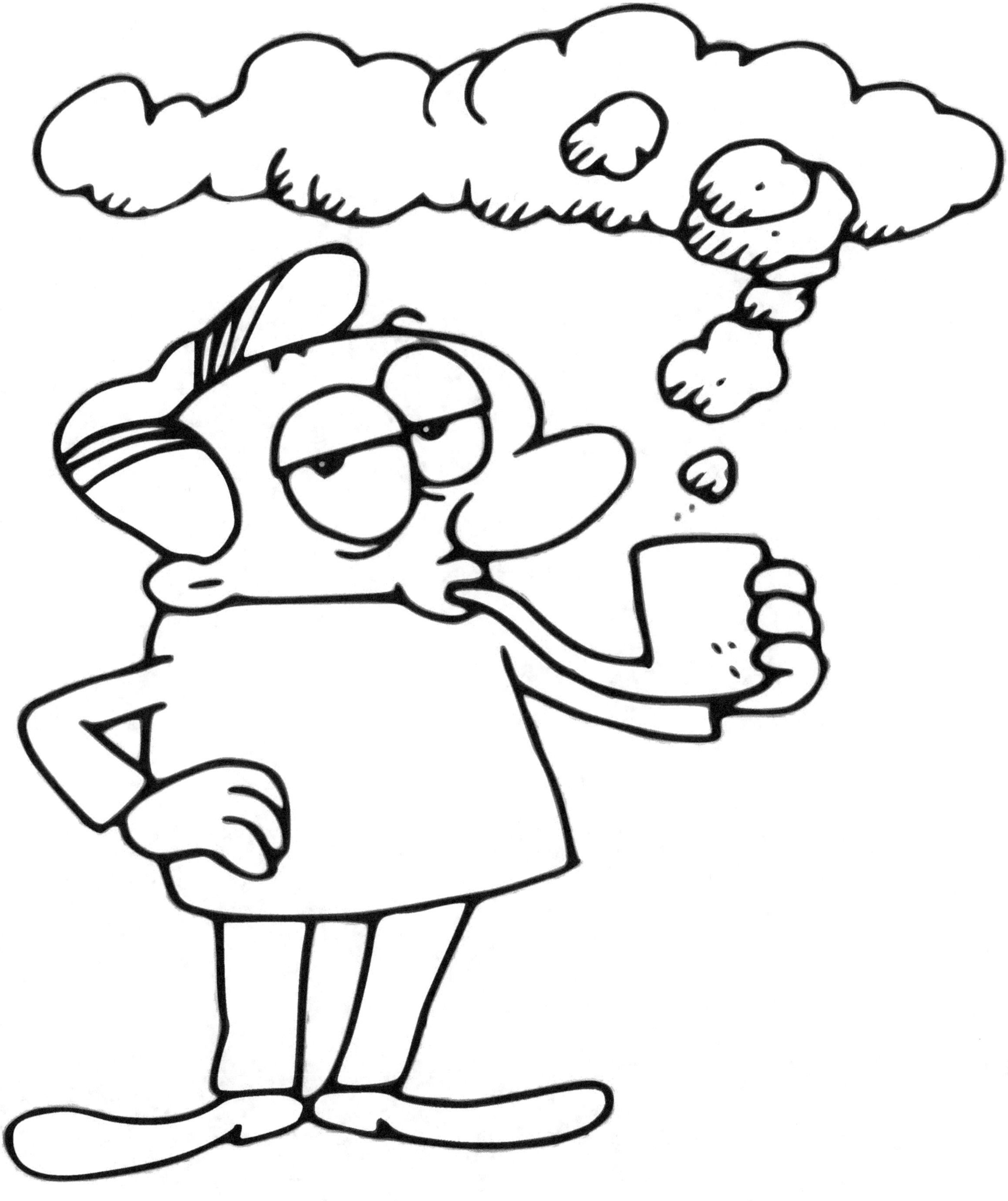

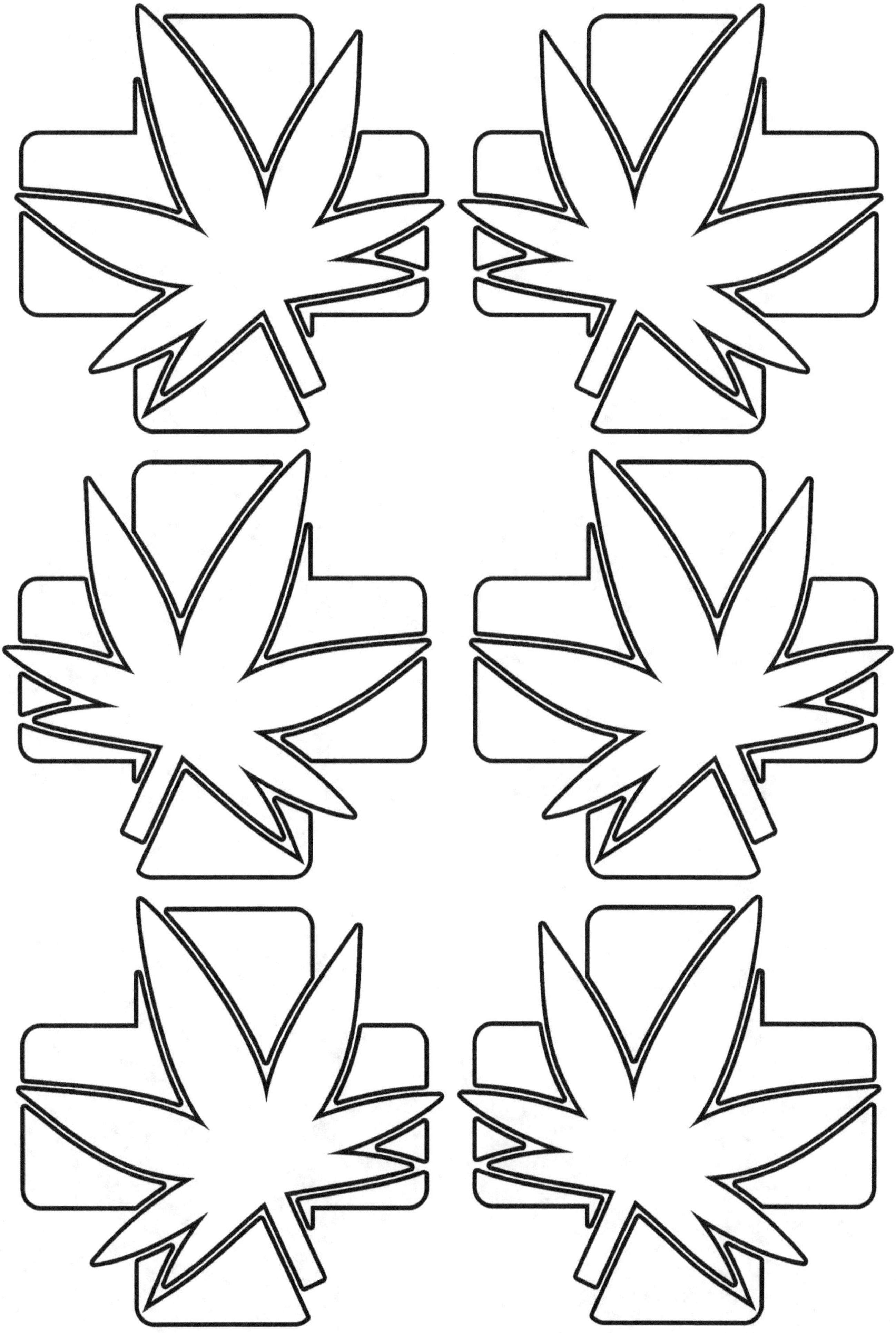

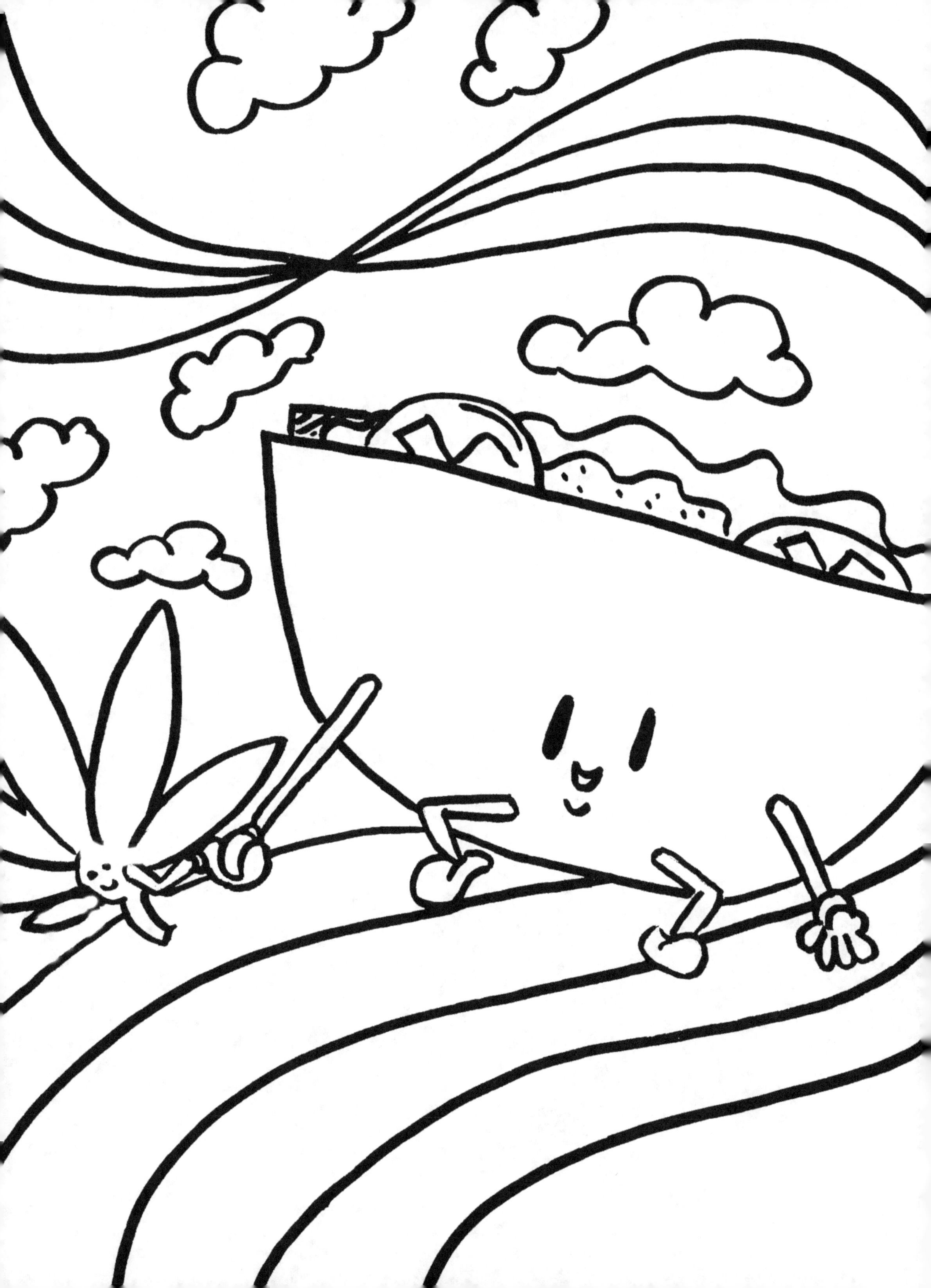

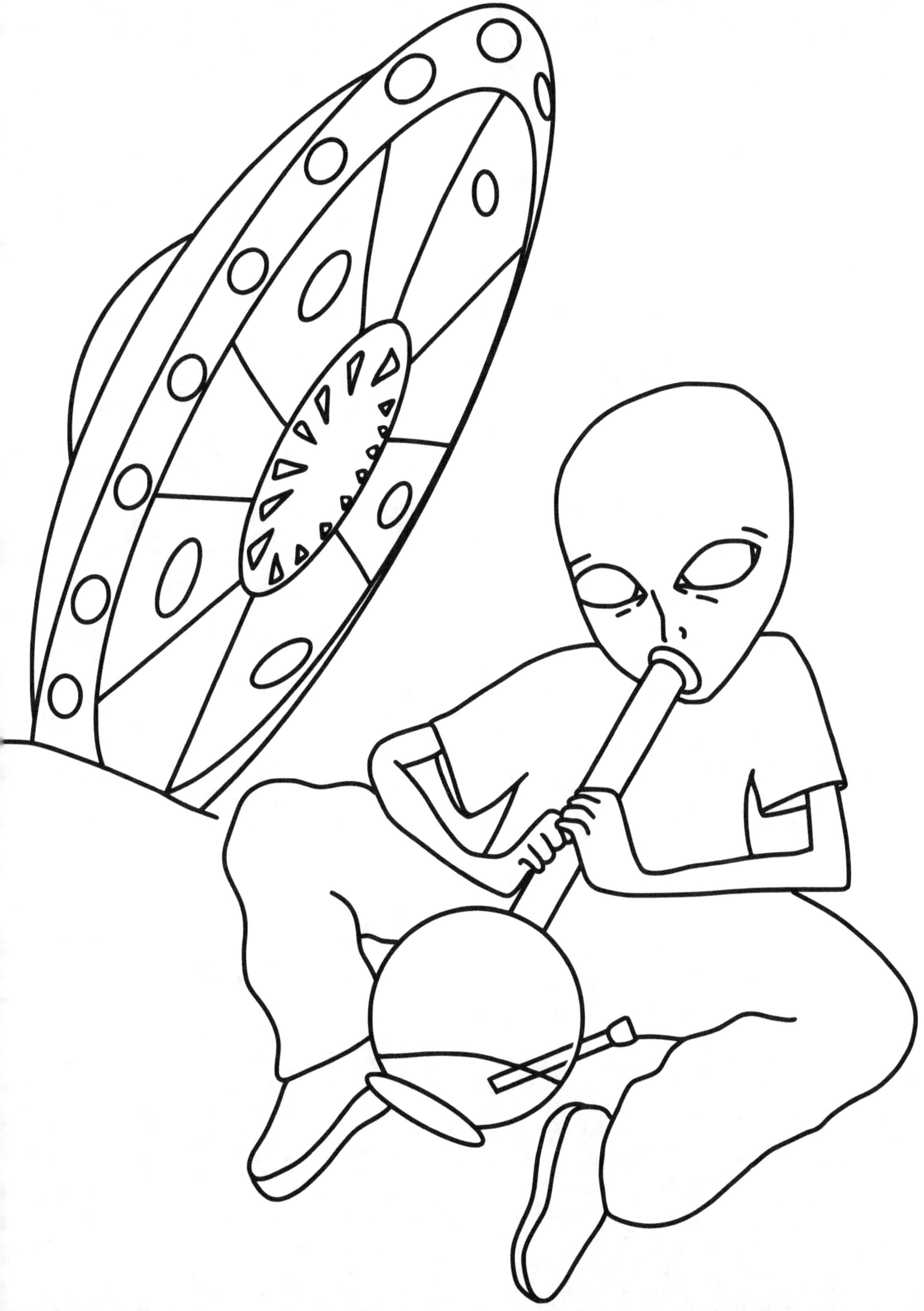

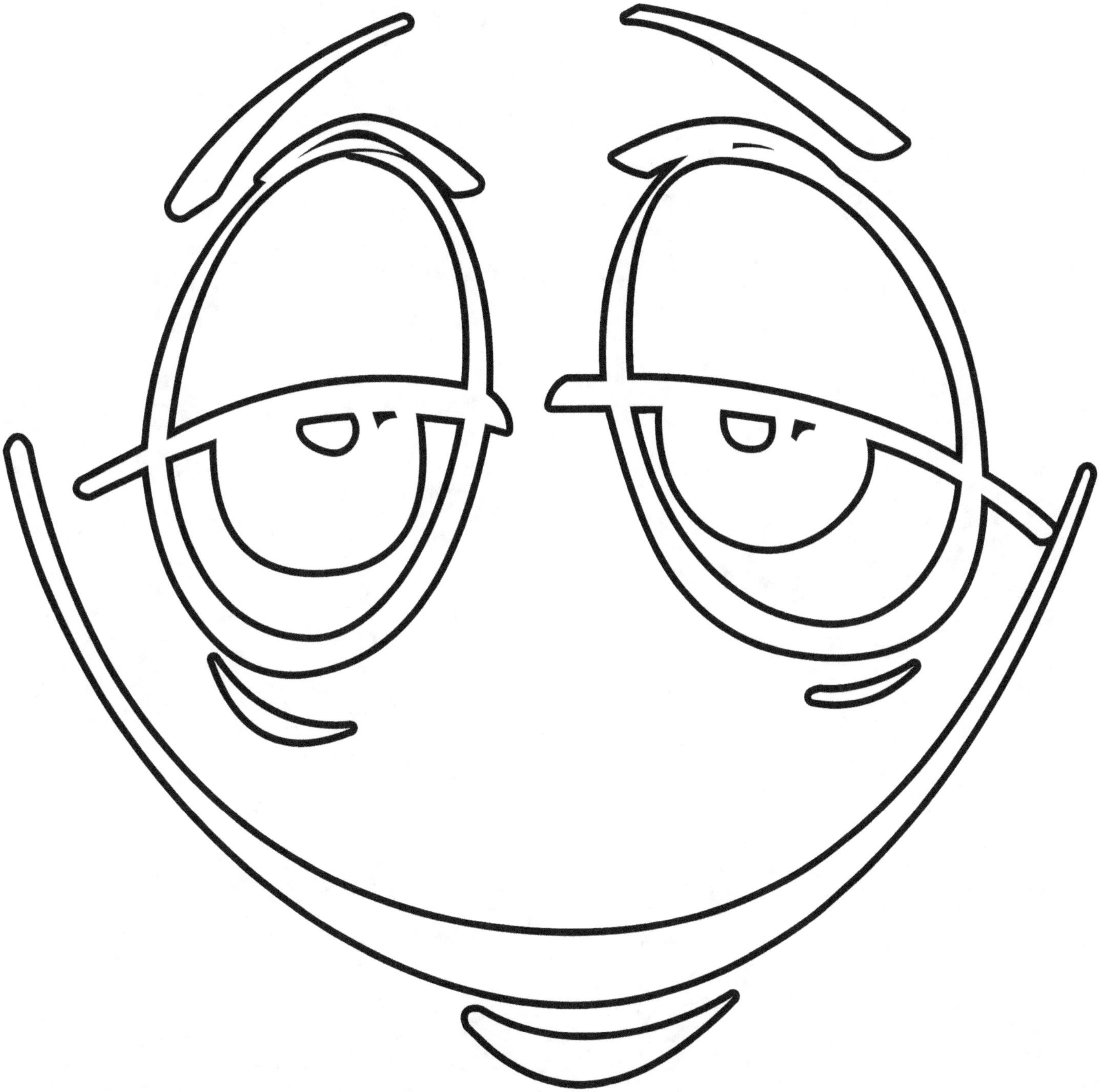

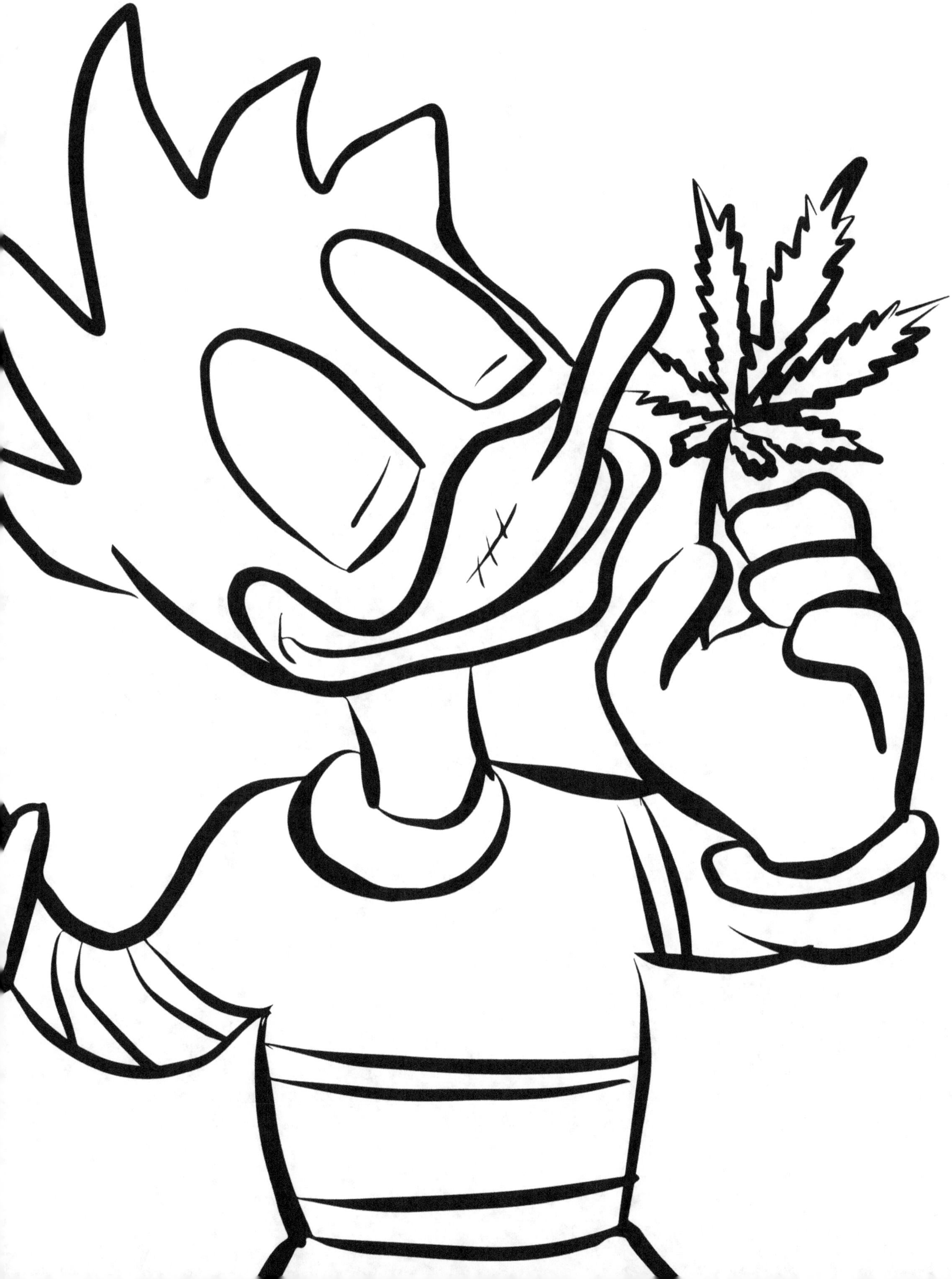

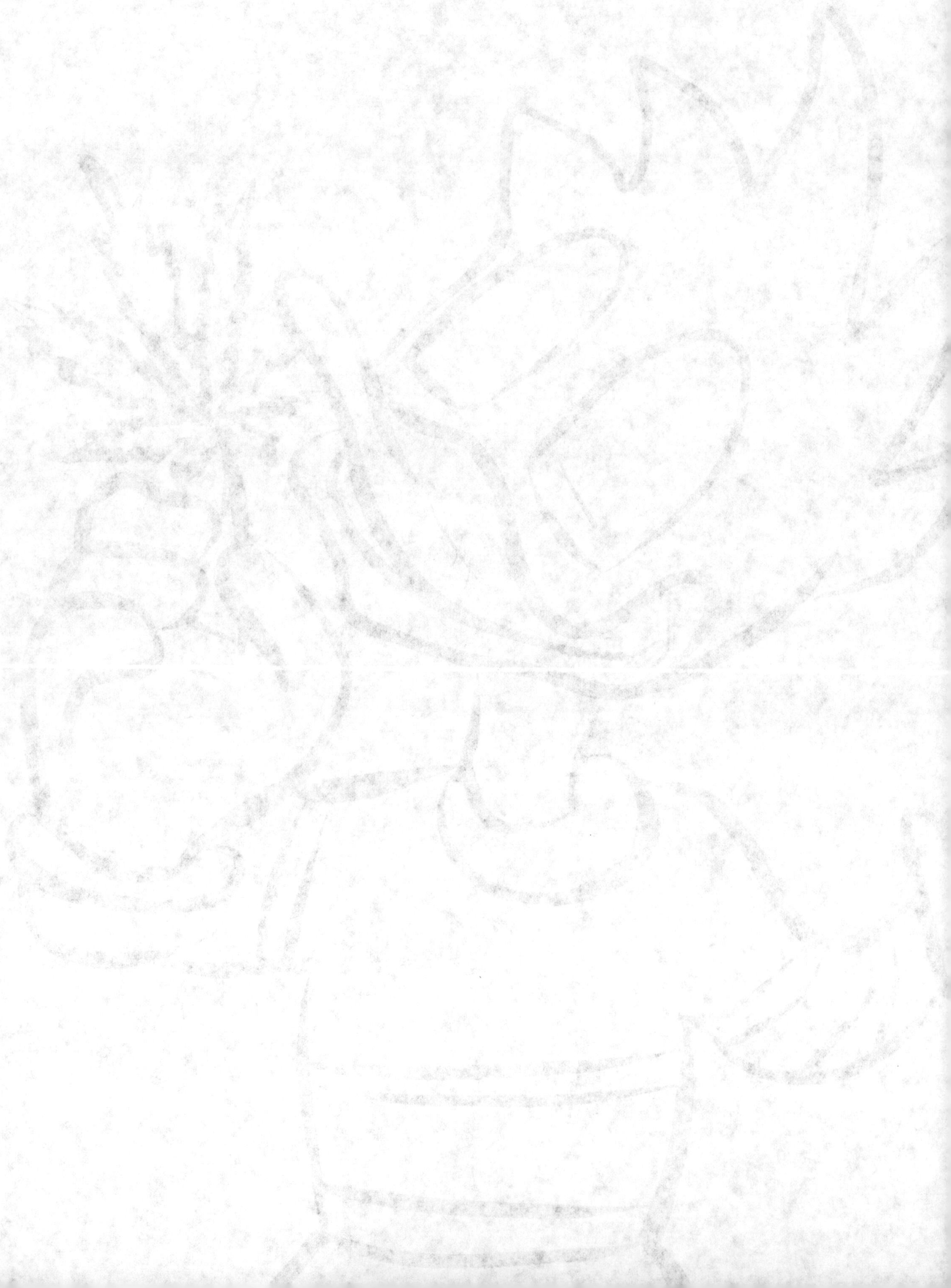

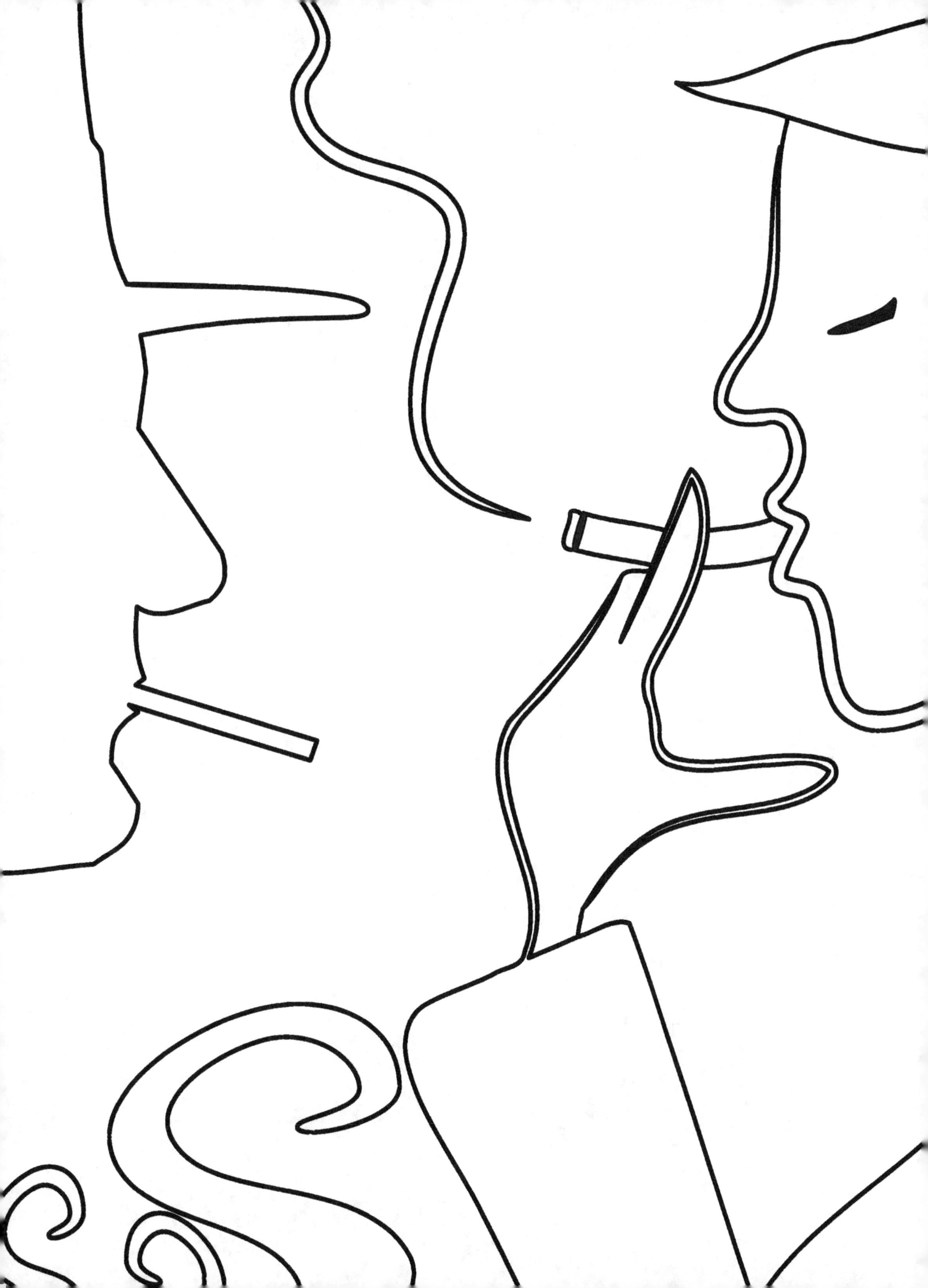

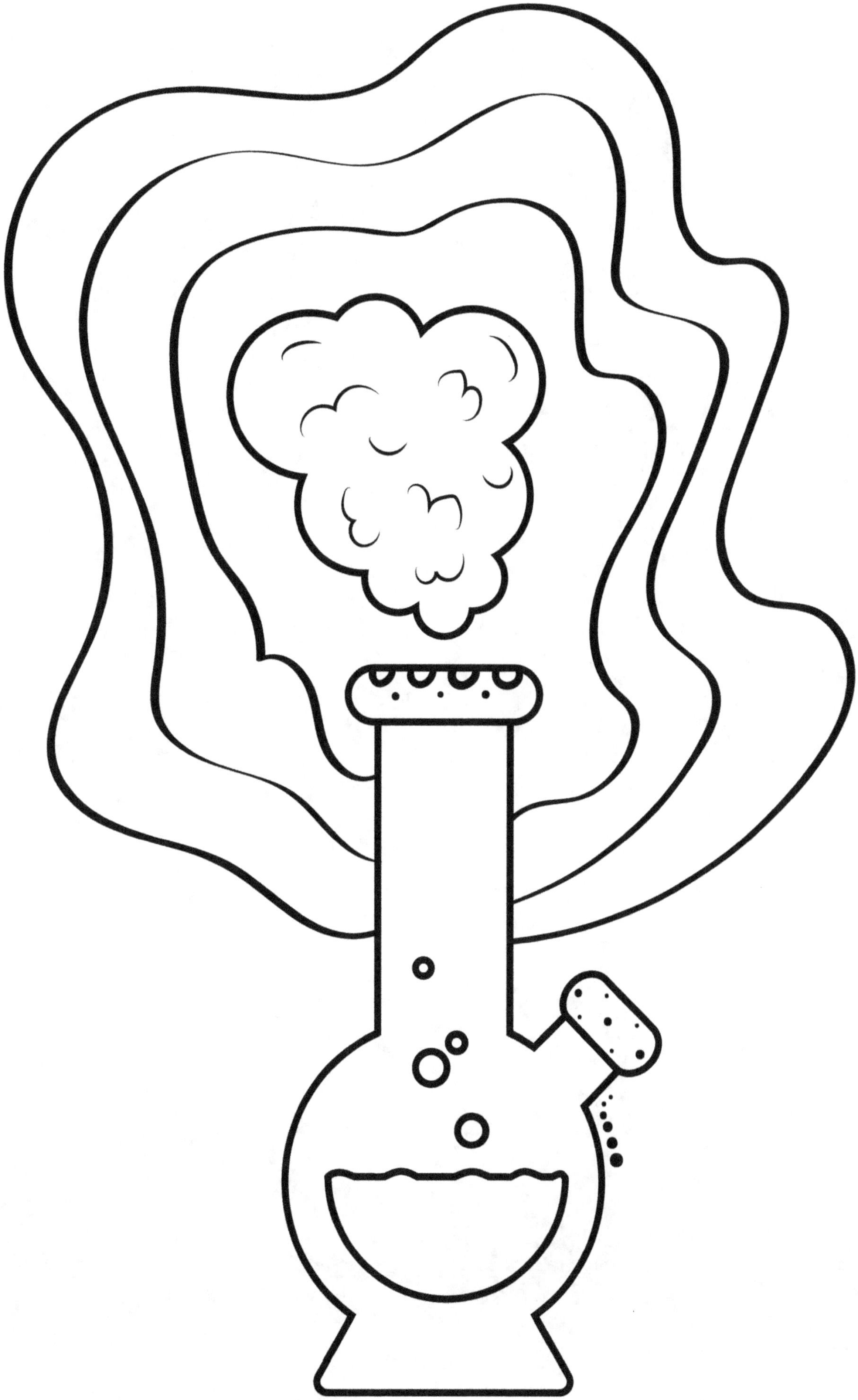

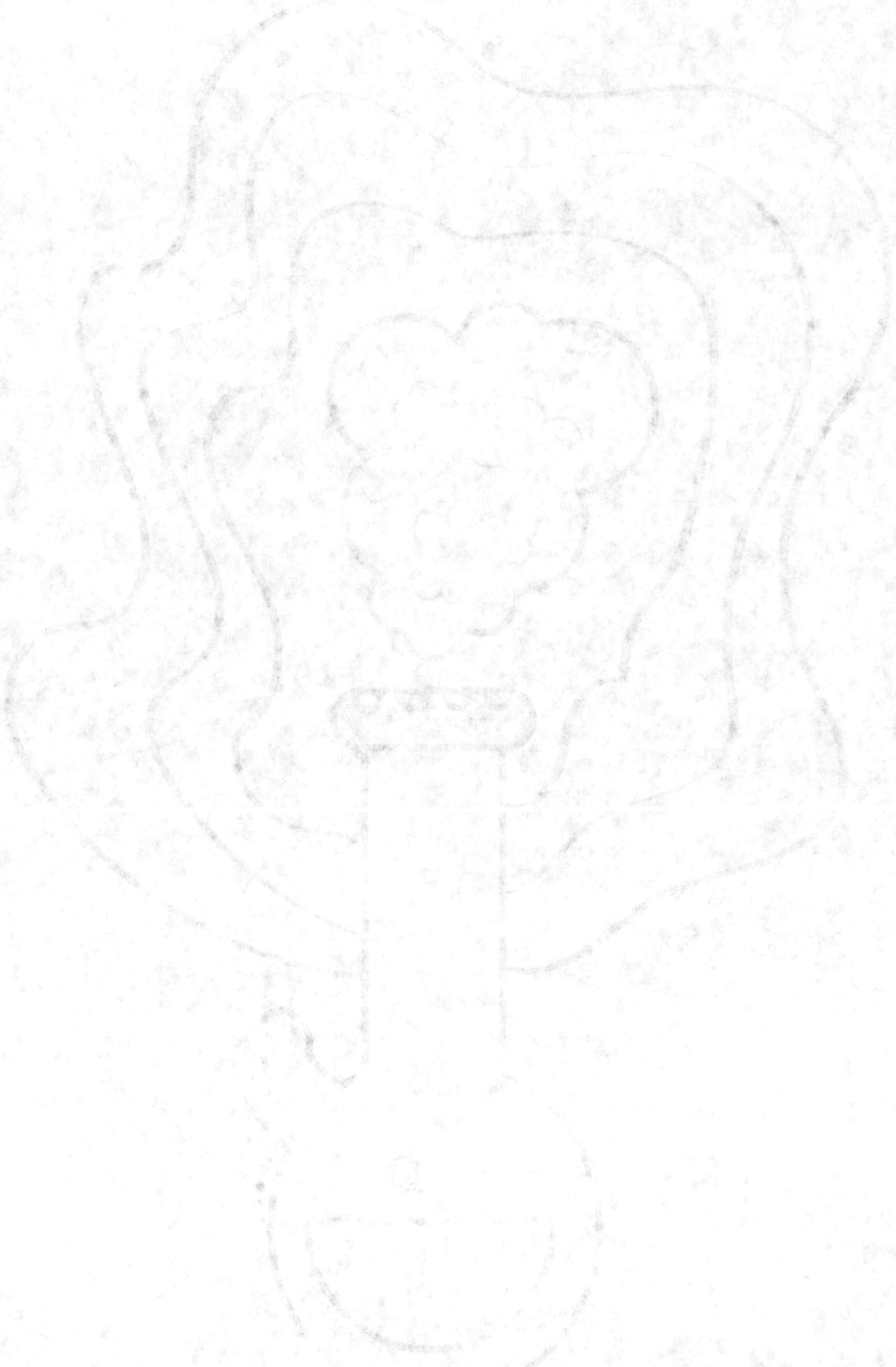

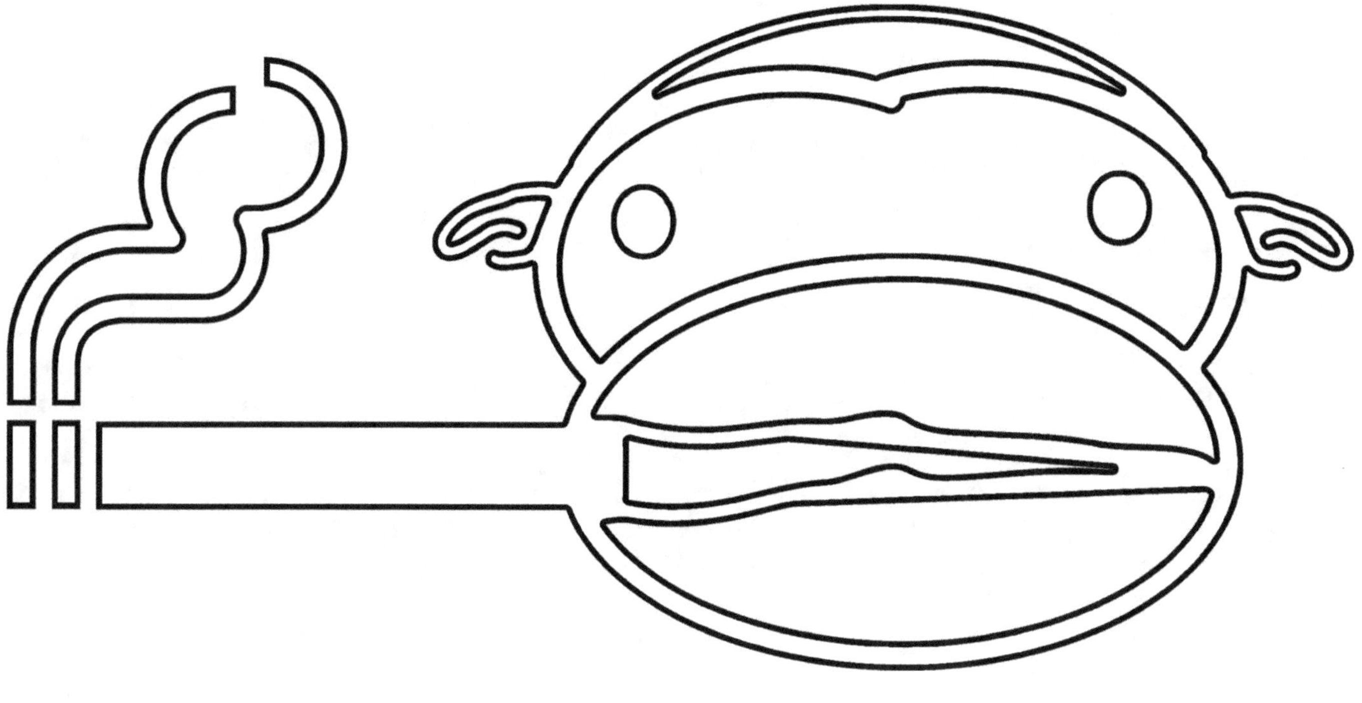

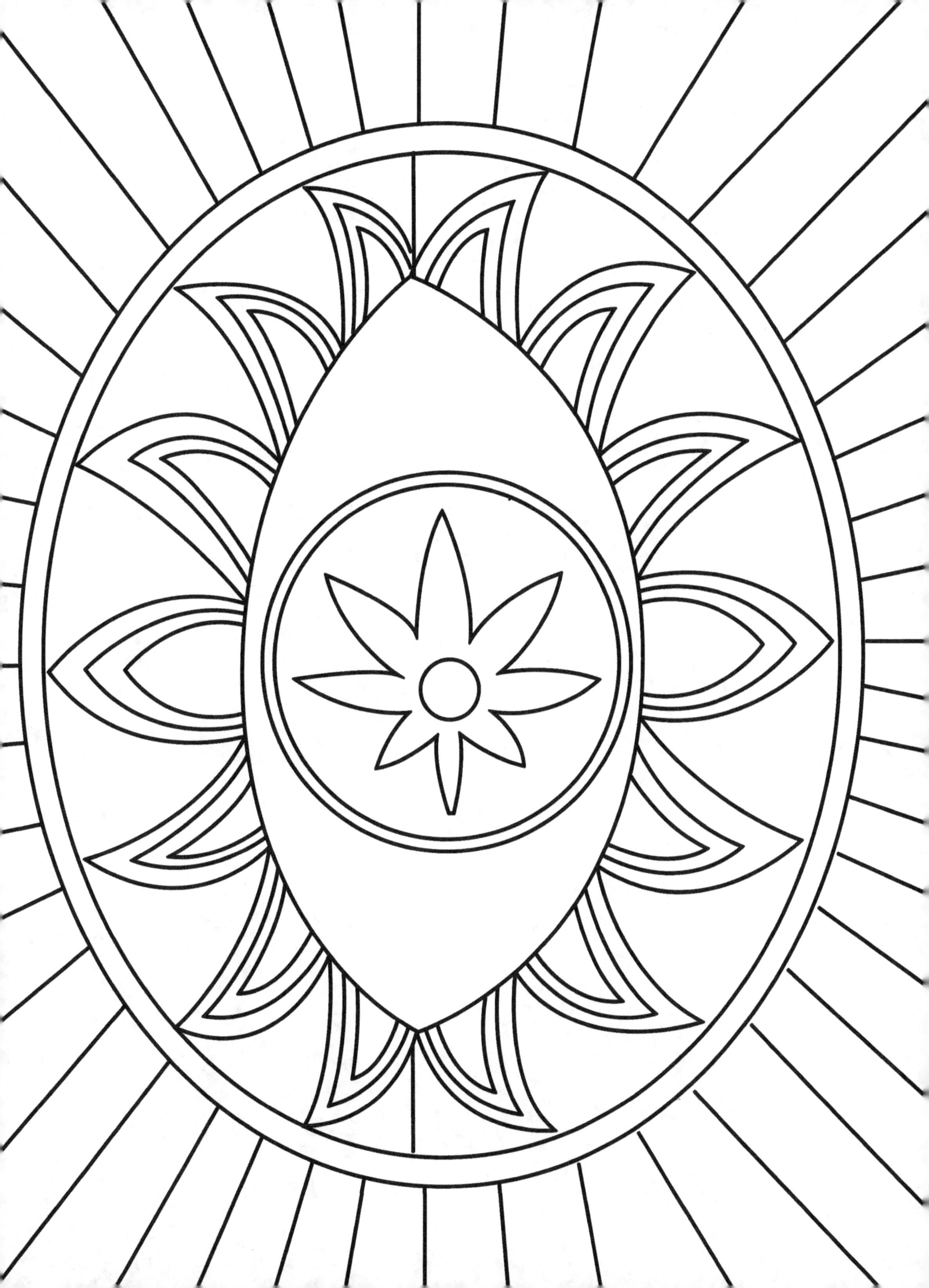

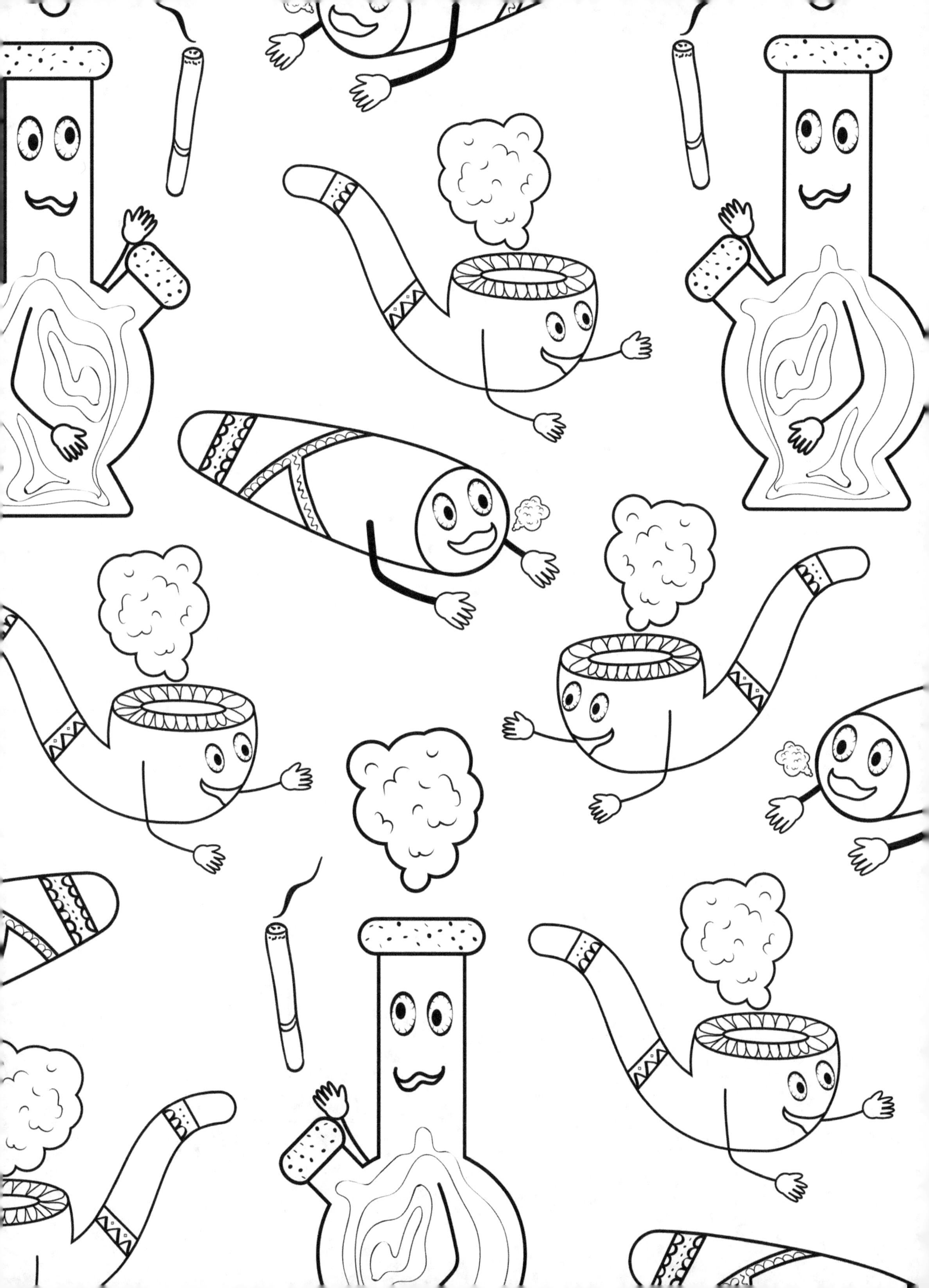

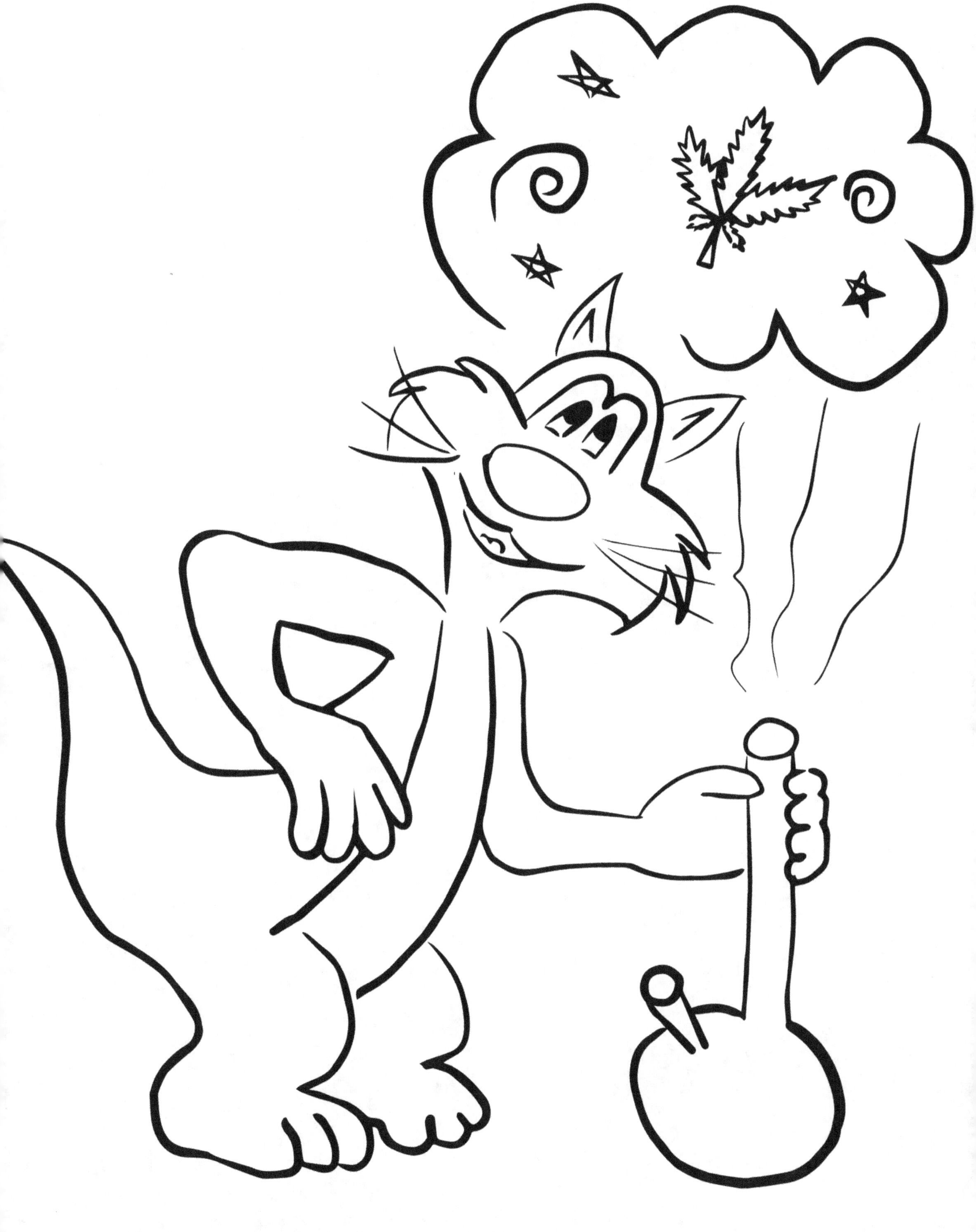

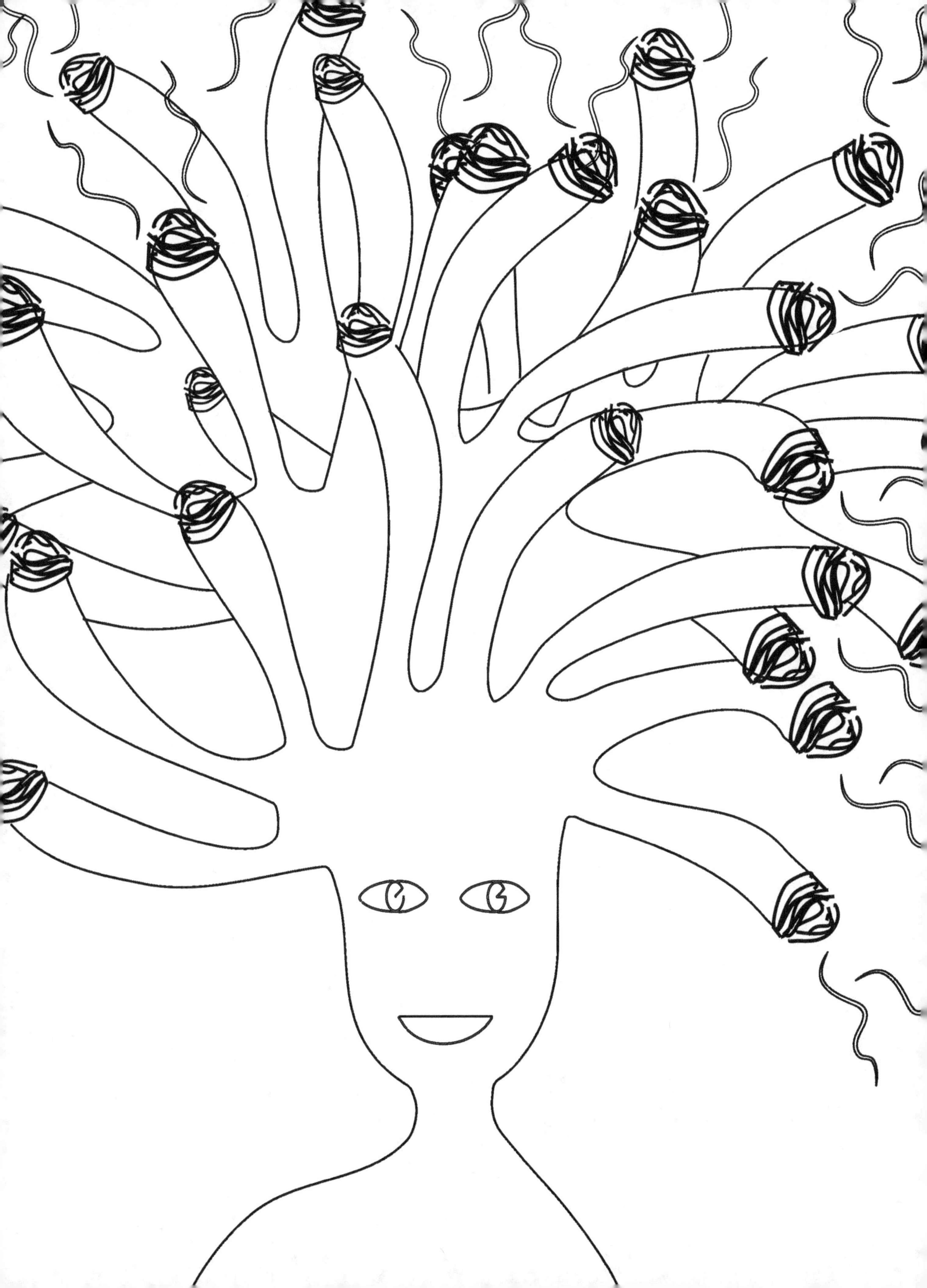

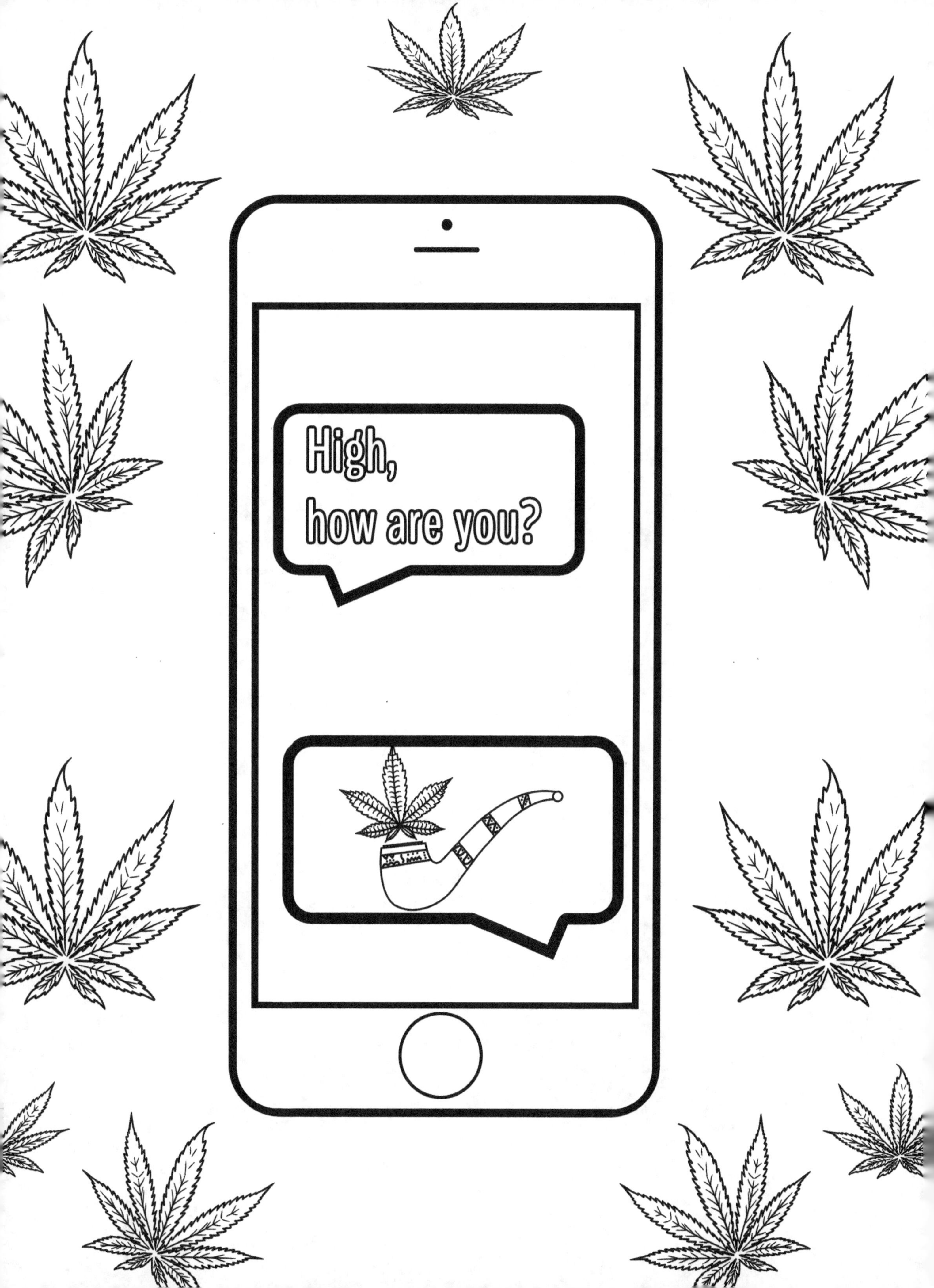
High,
how are you?

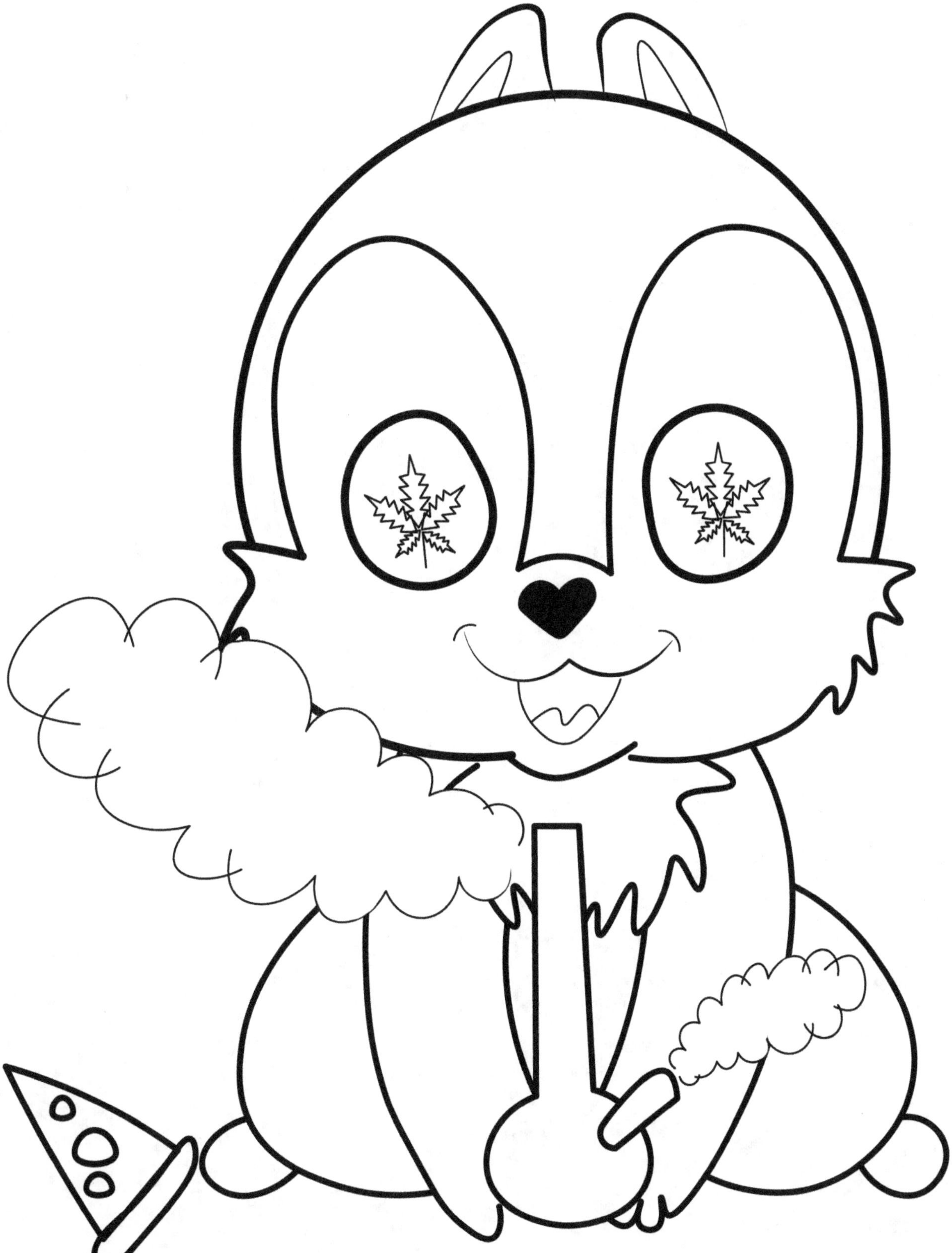

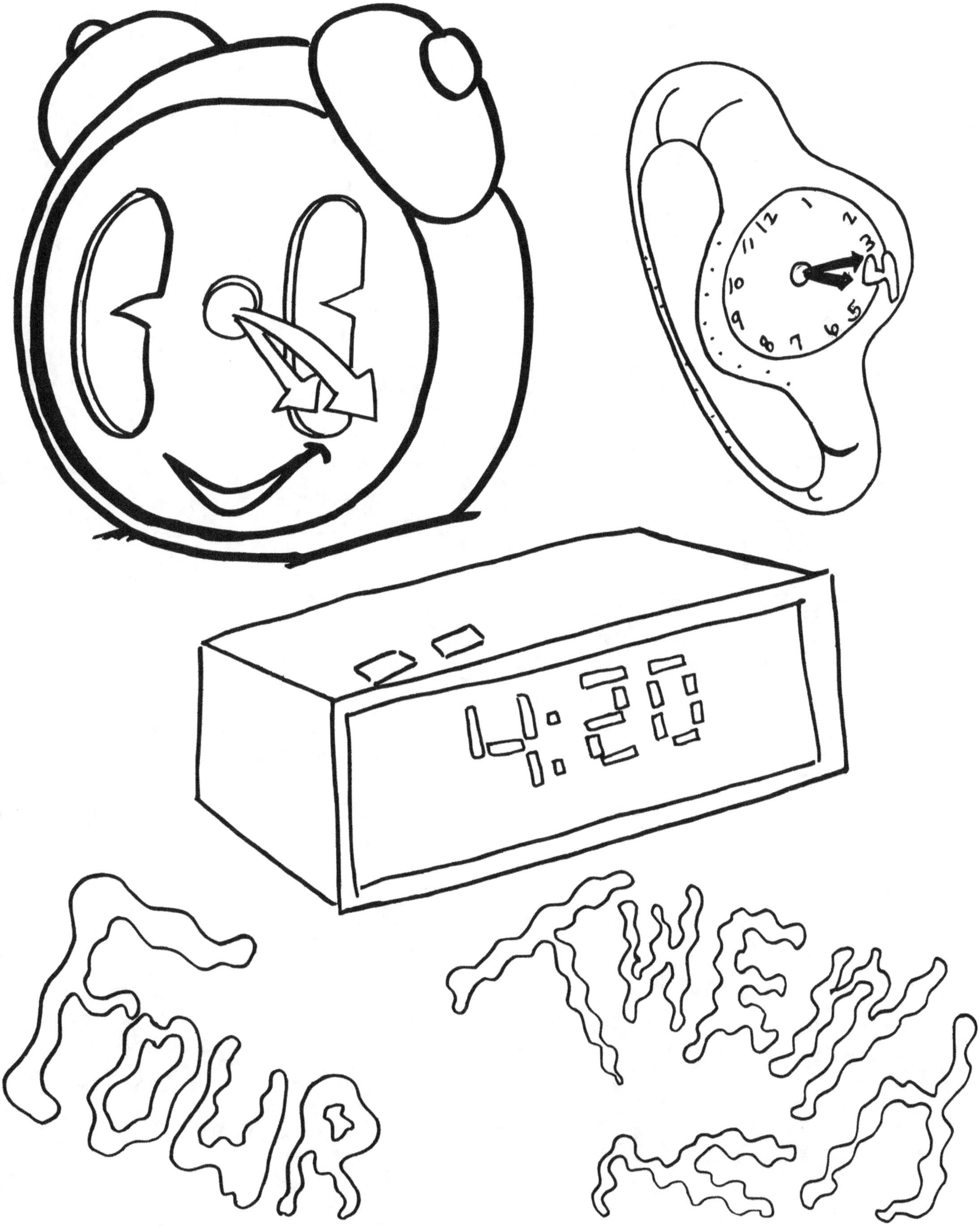
4:20
FOUR
TWENTY

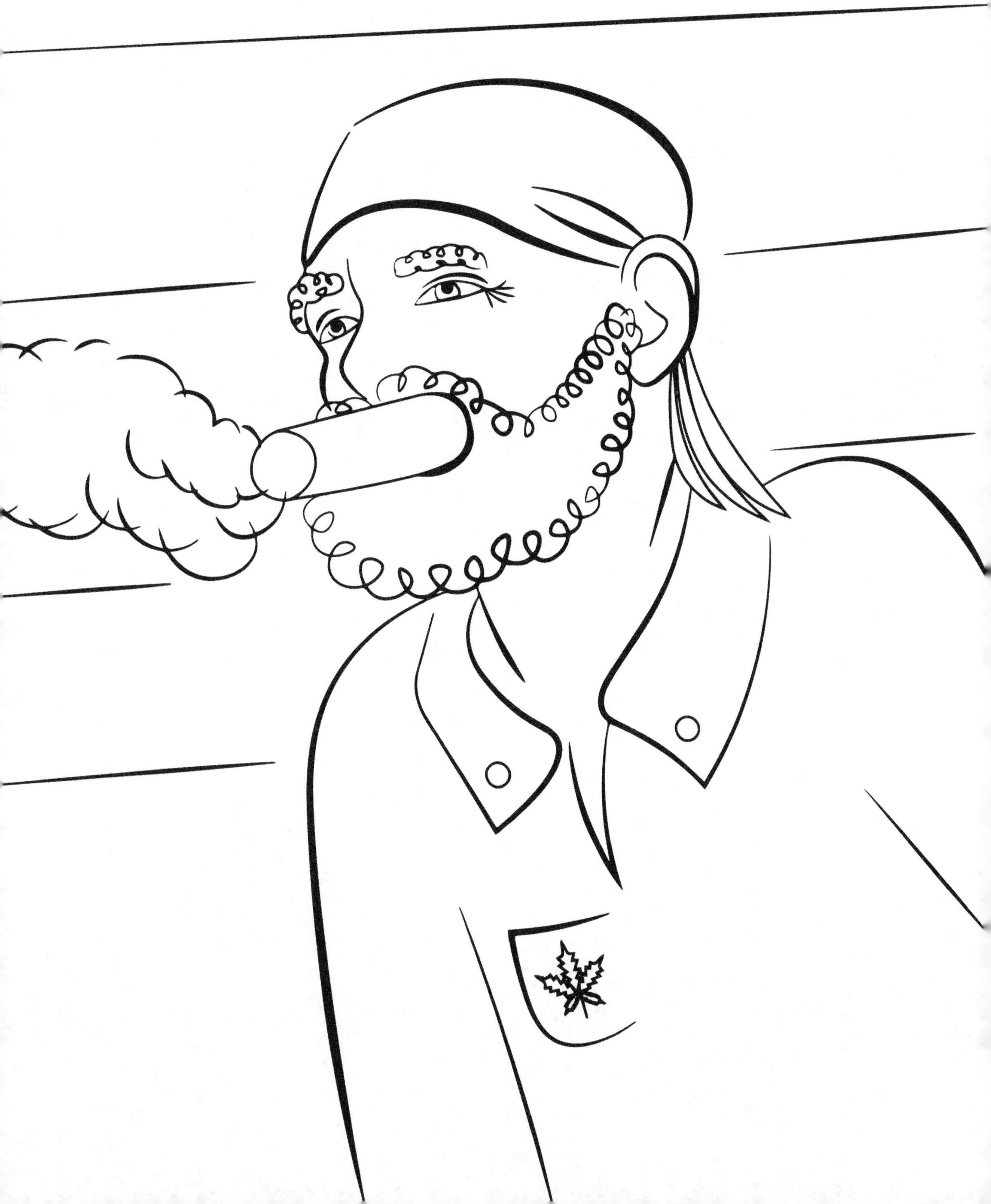

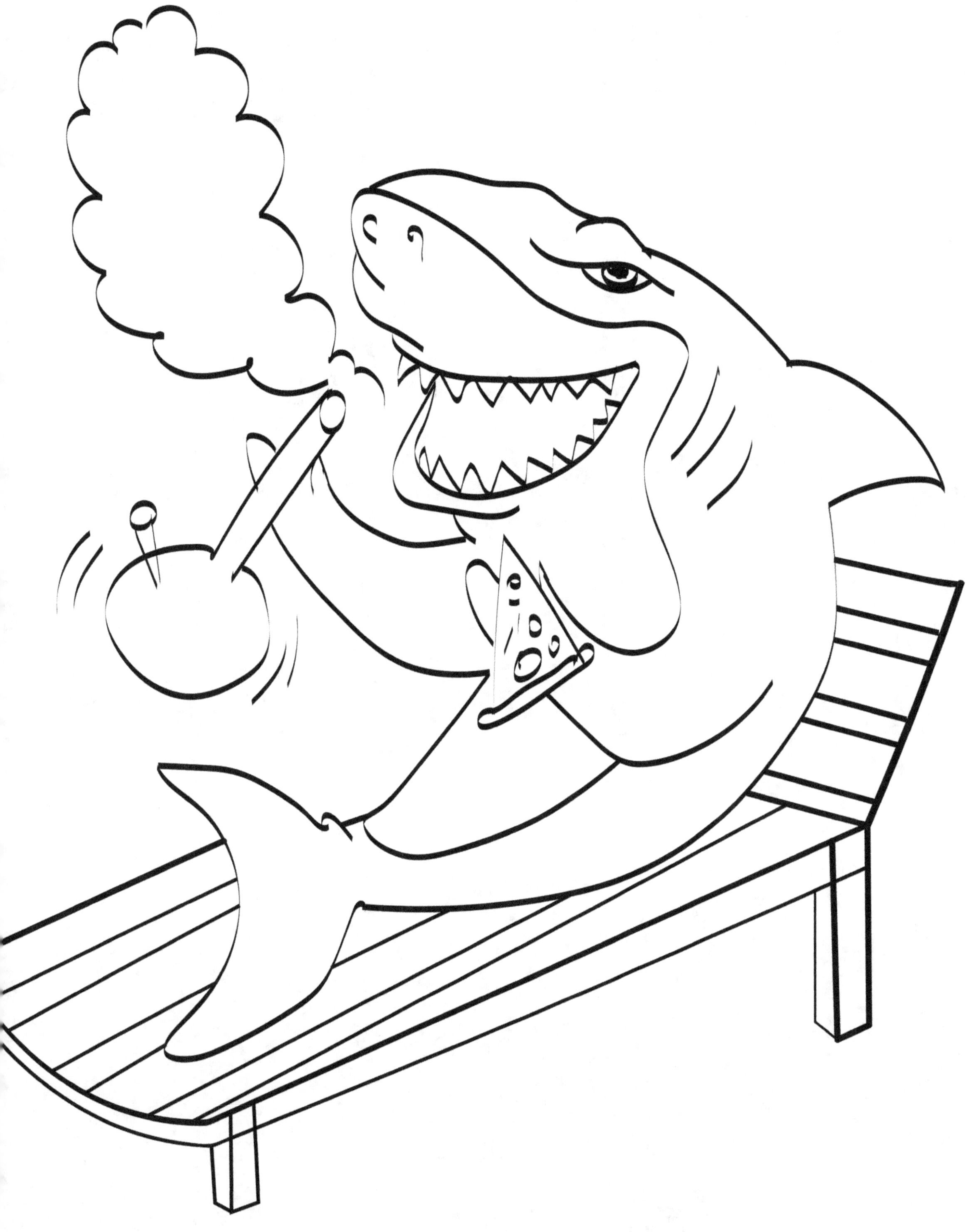

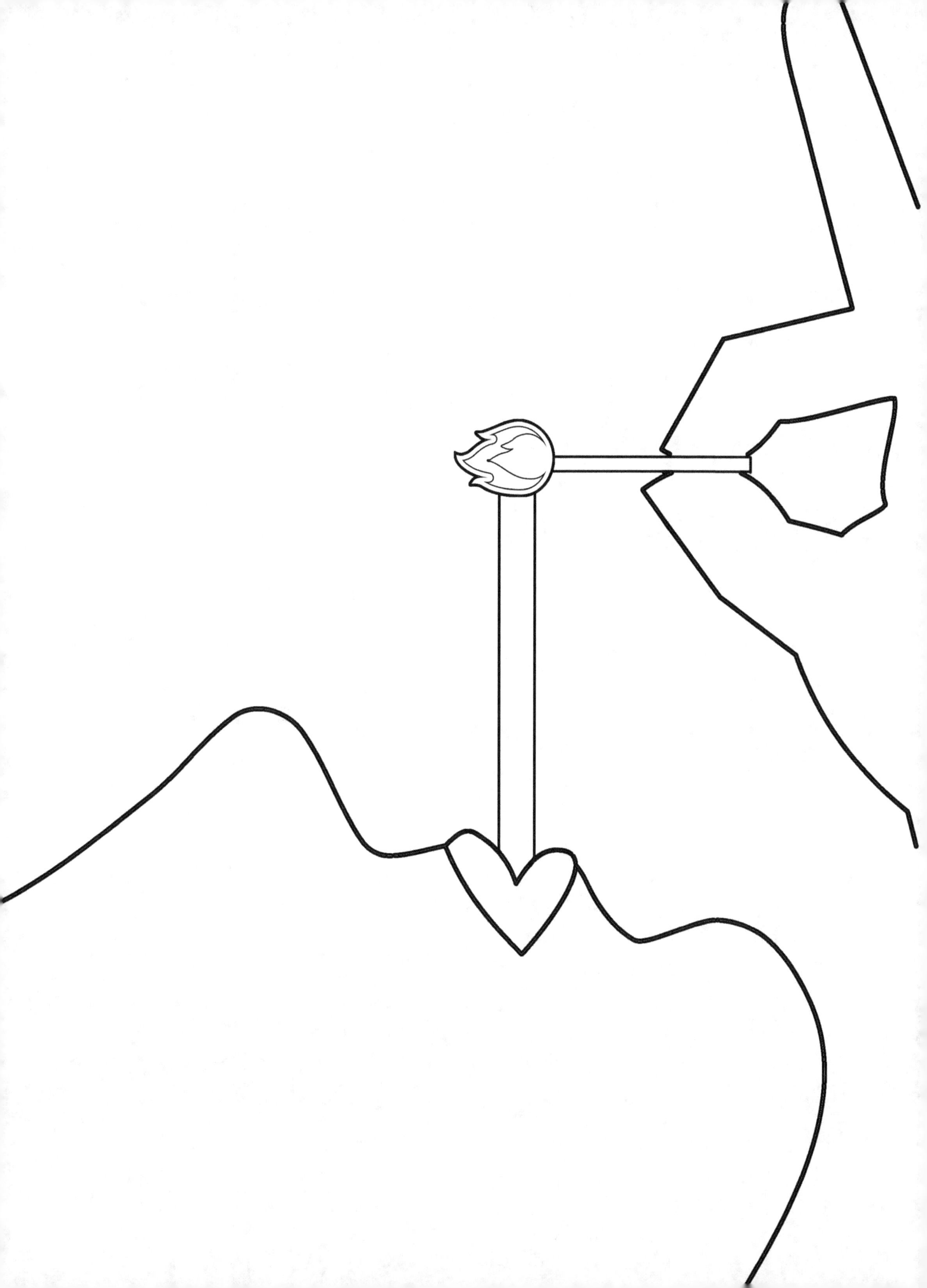

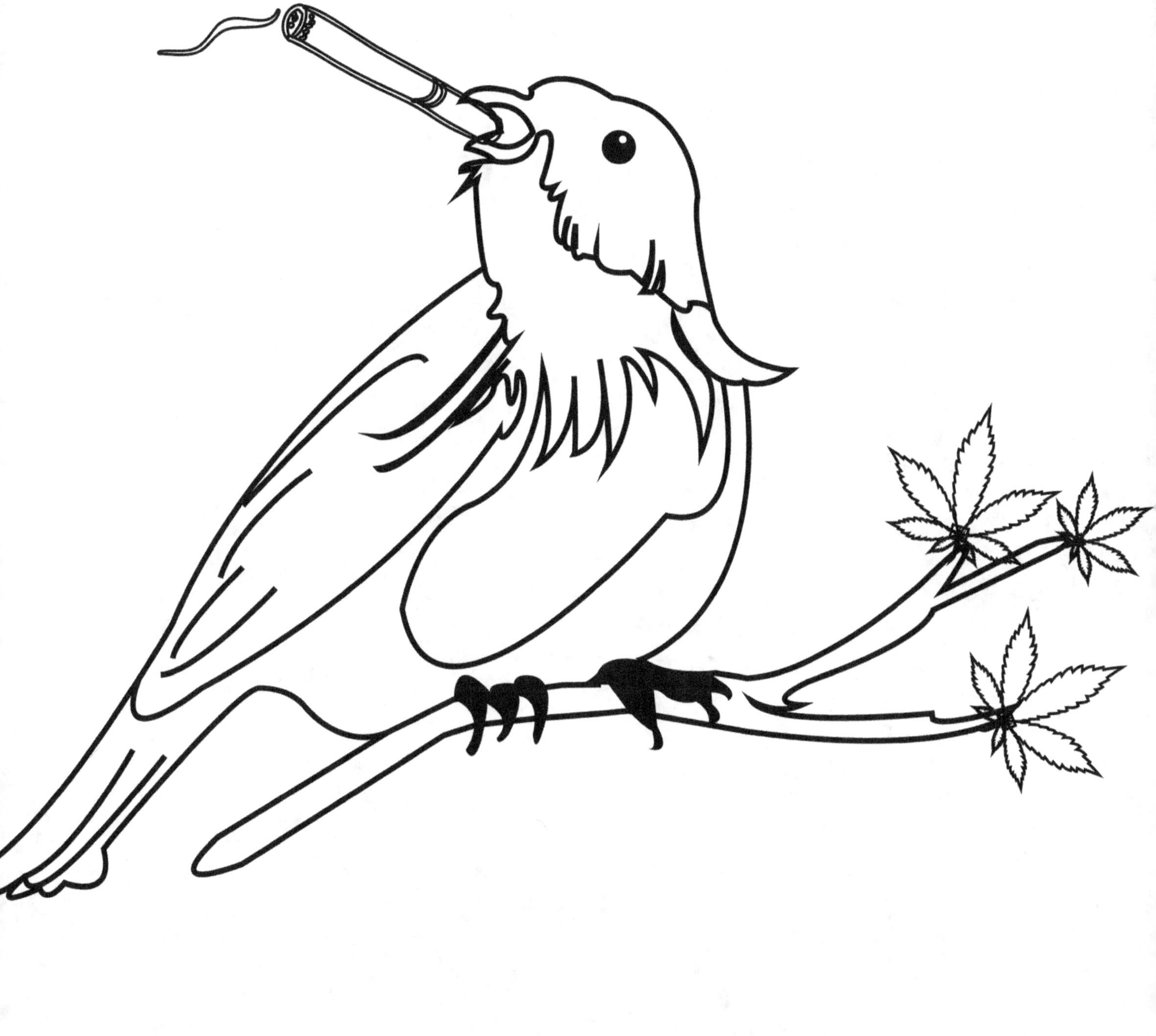

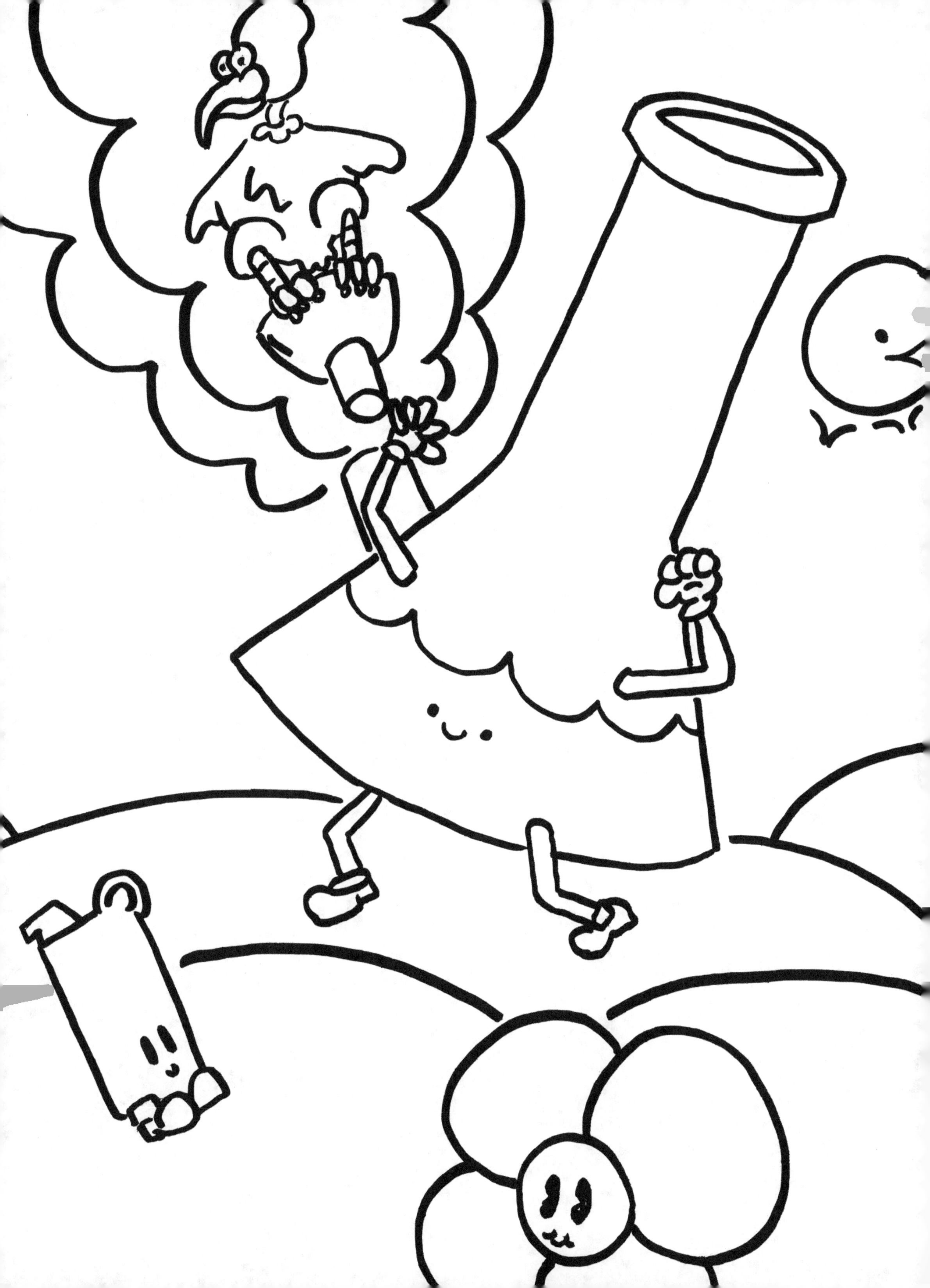

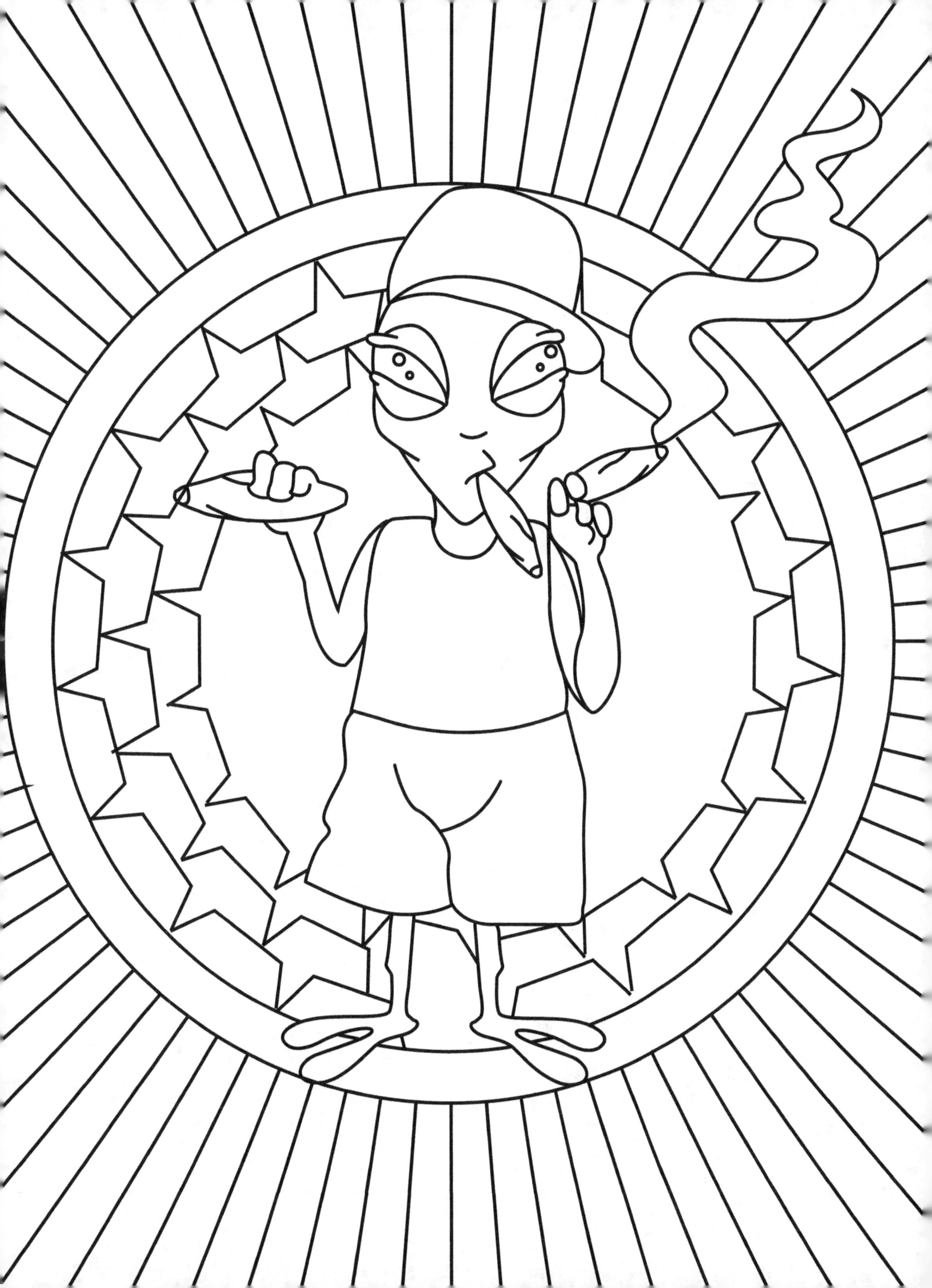

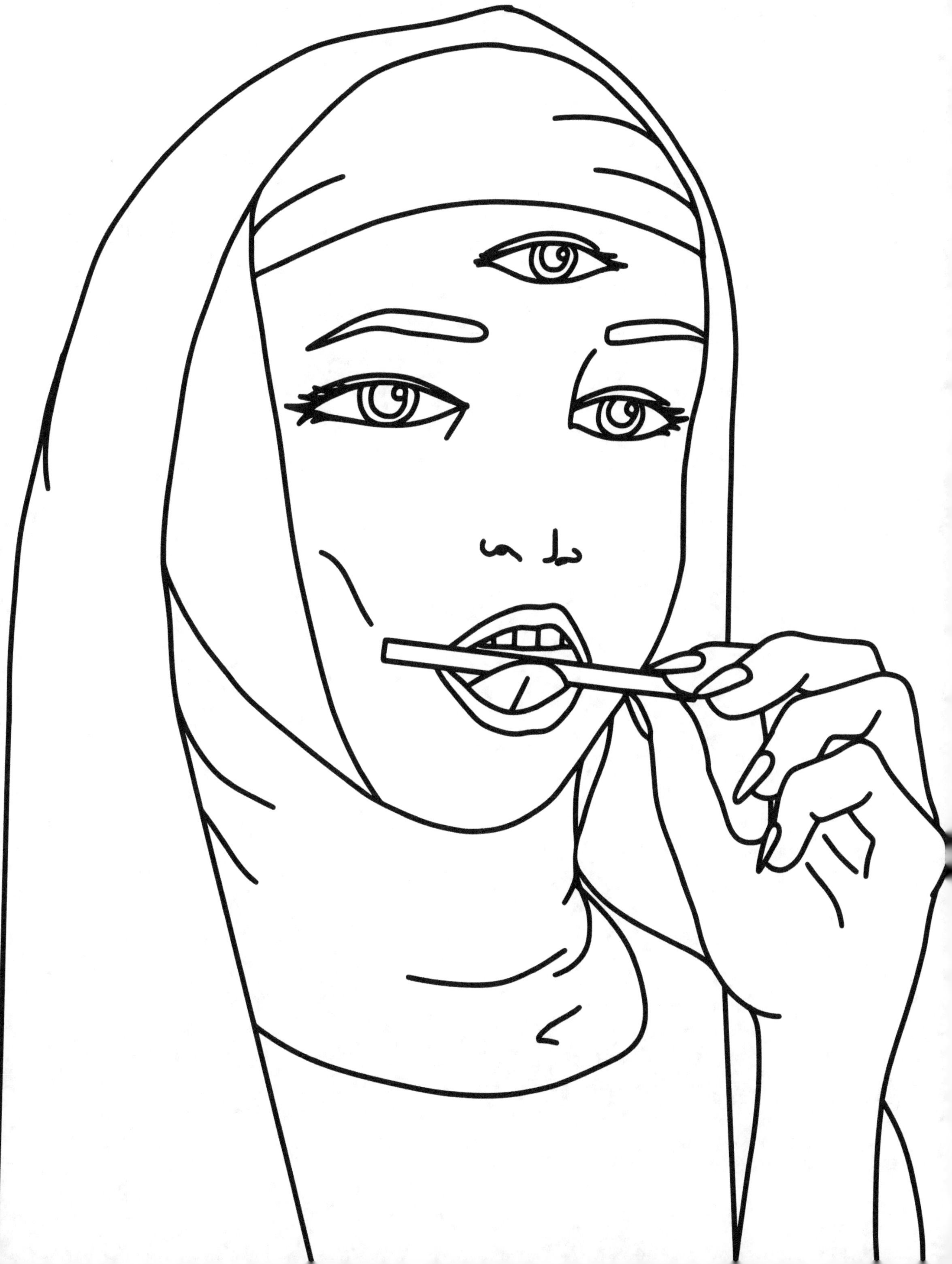

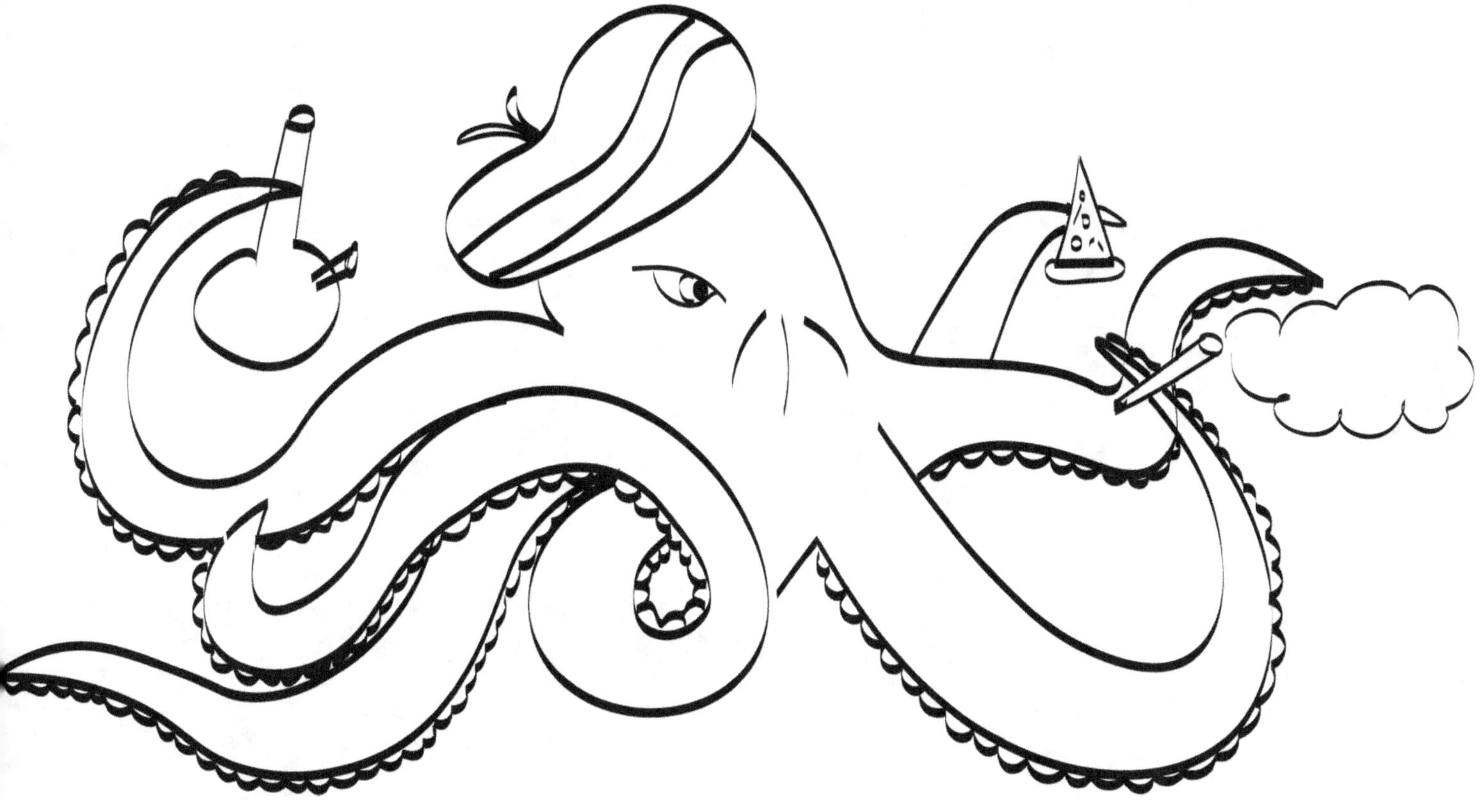

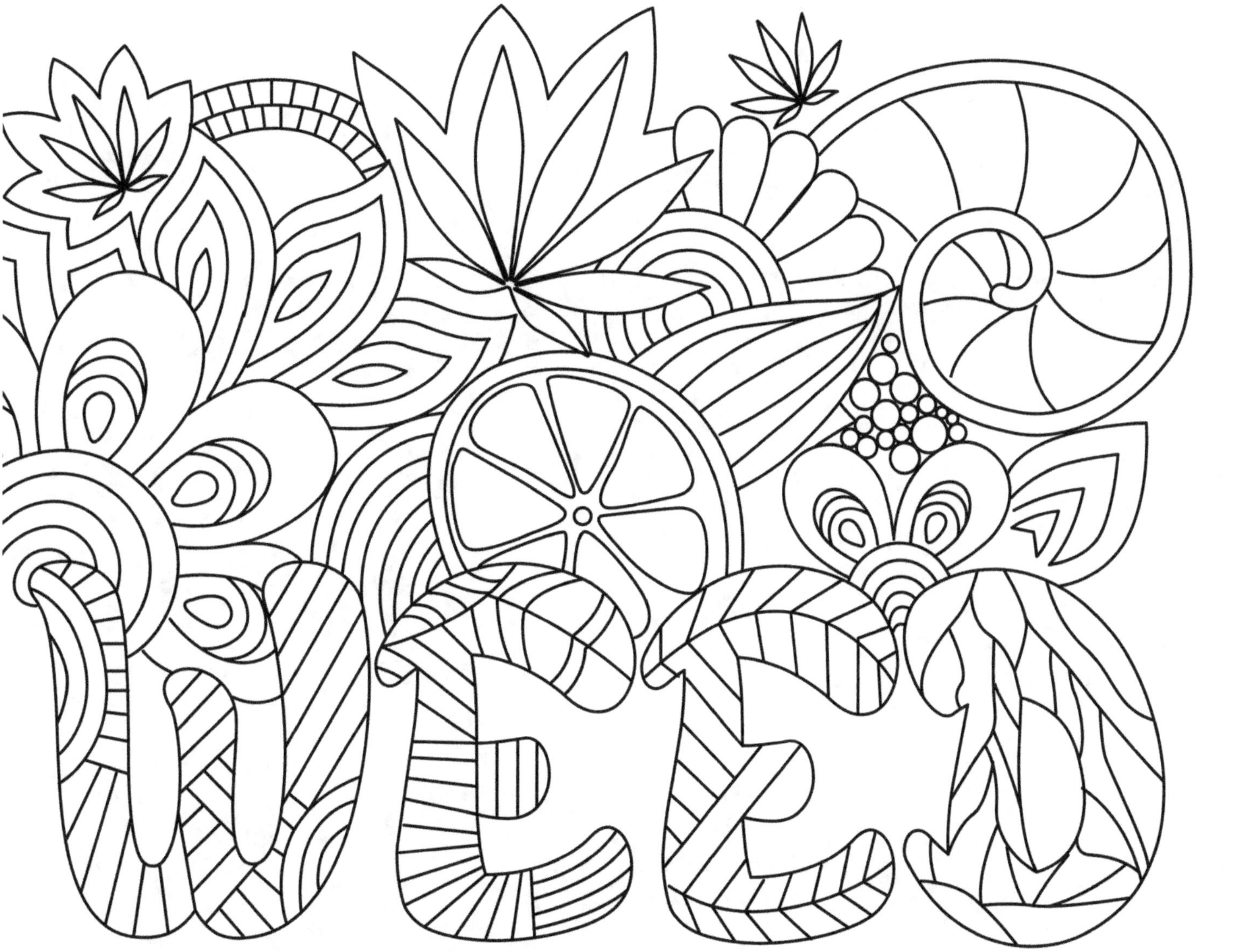
WEED

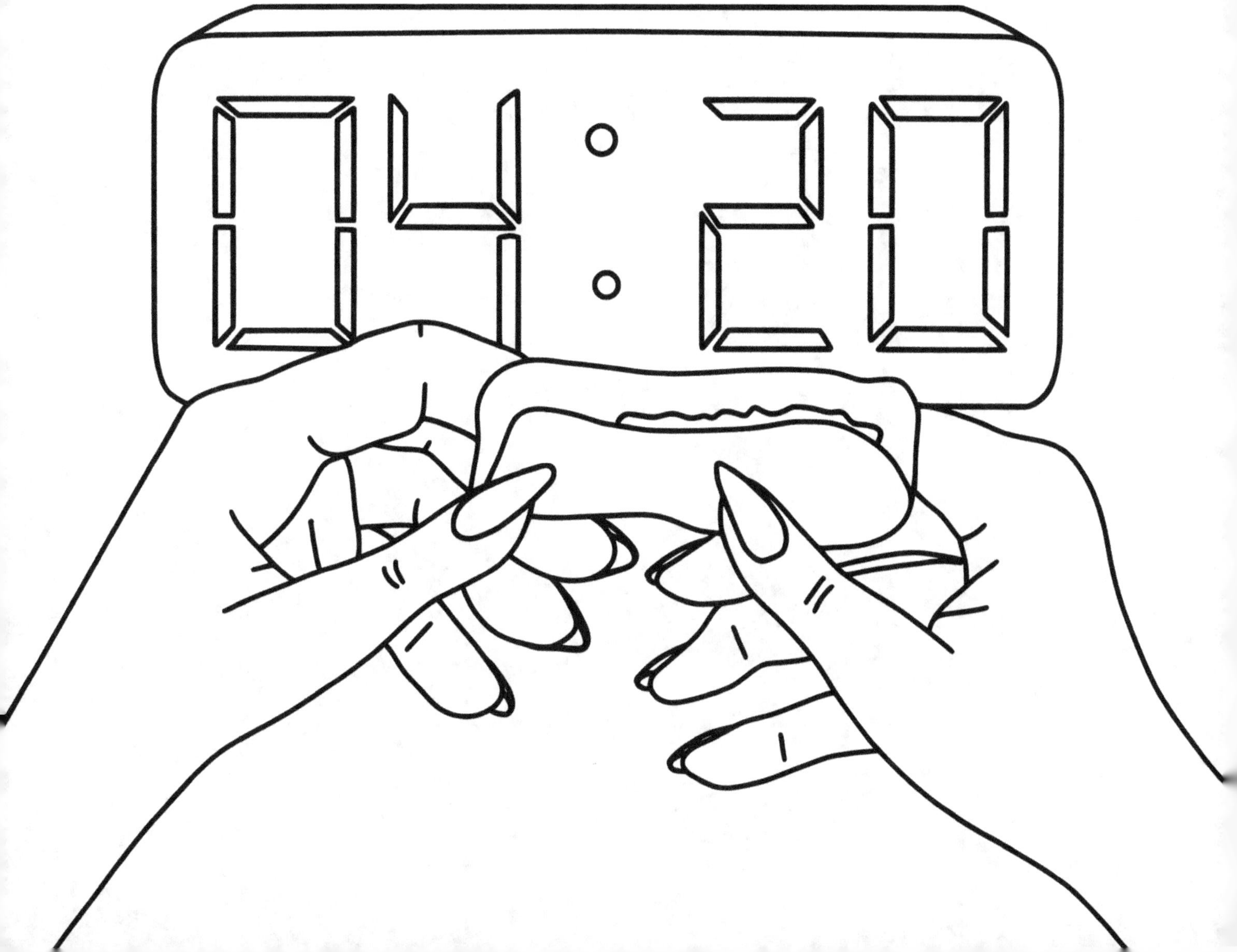
04:20

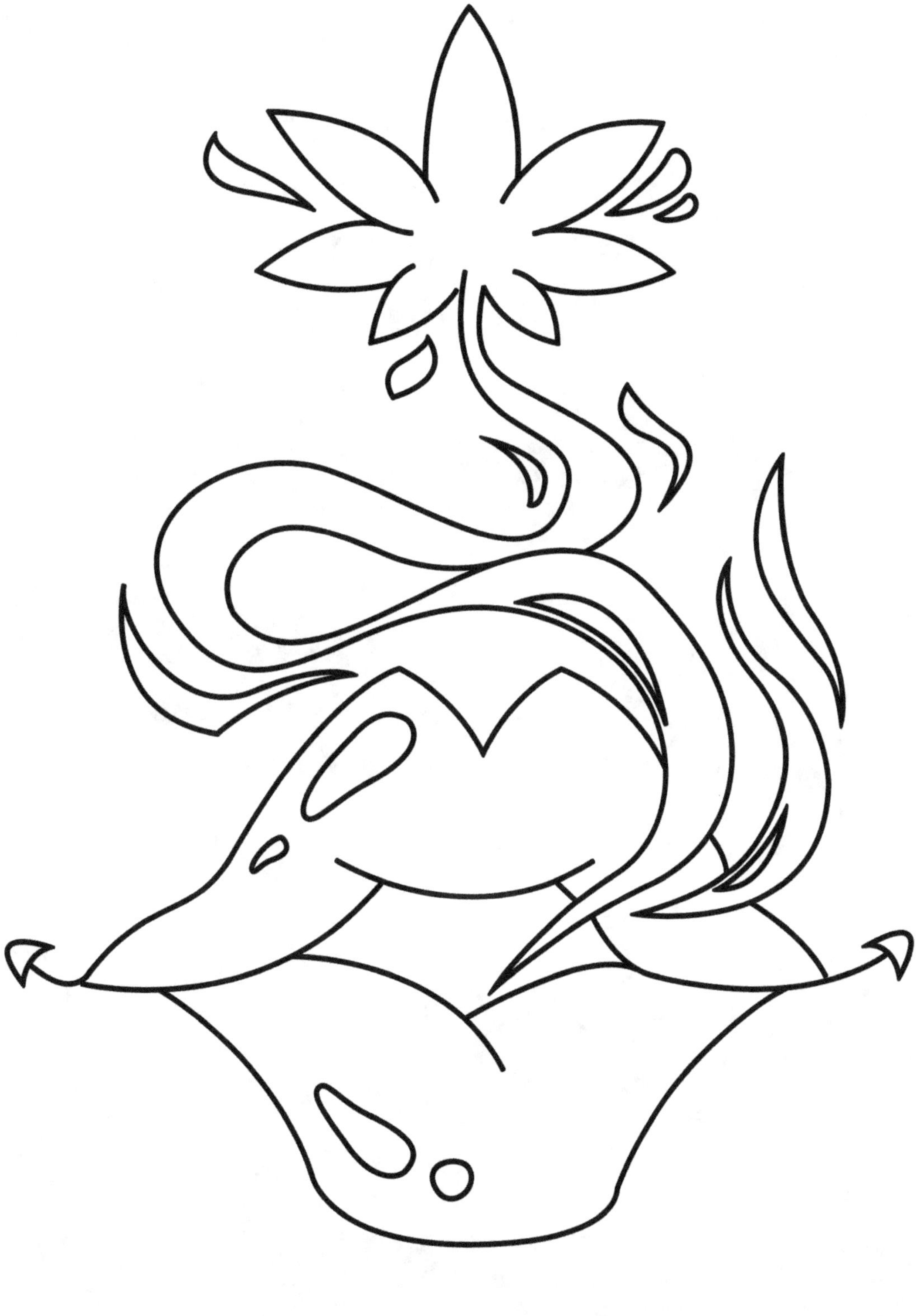

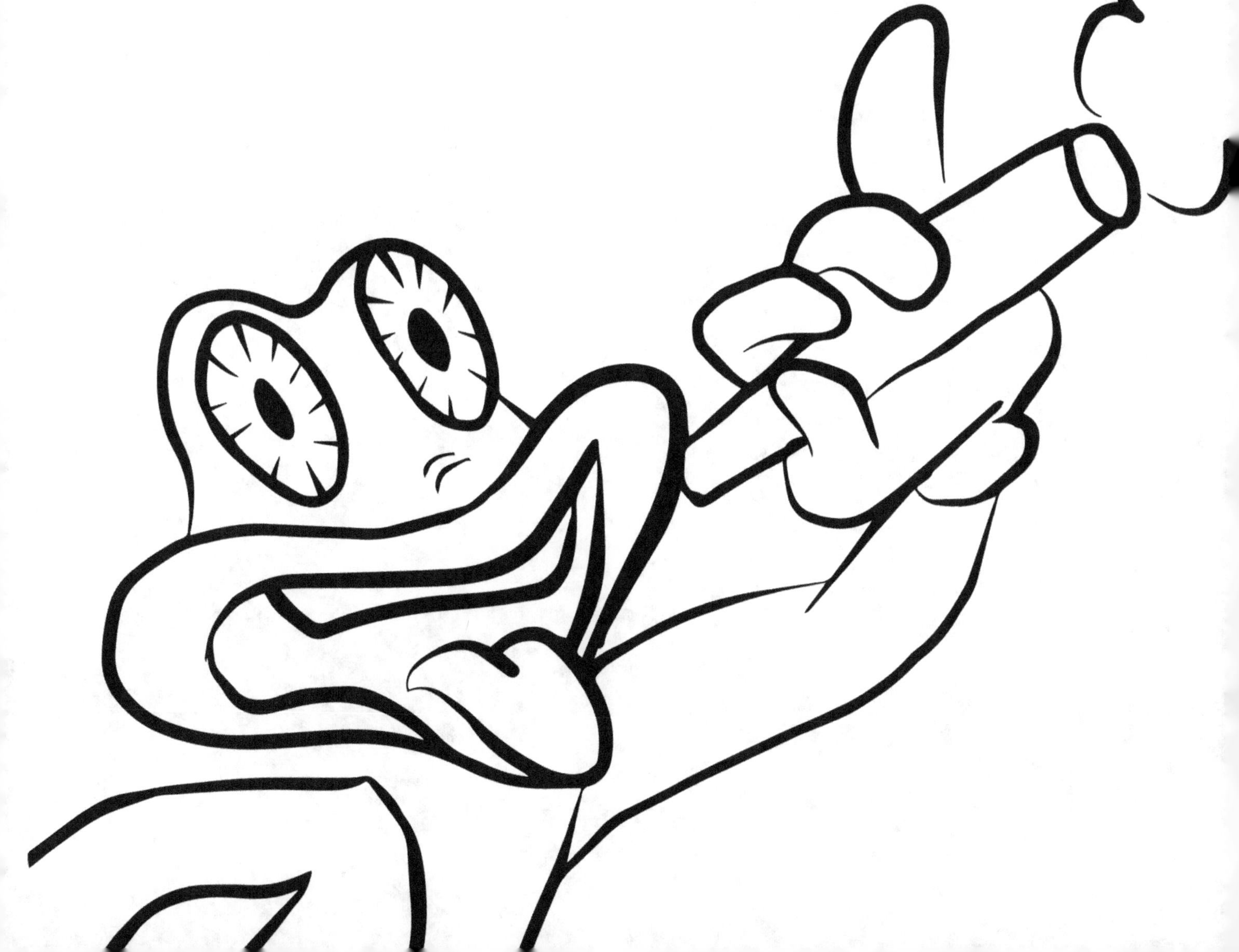

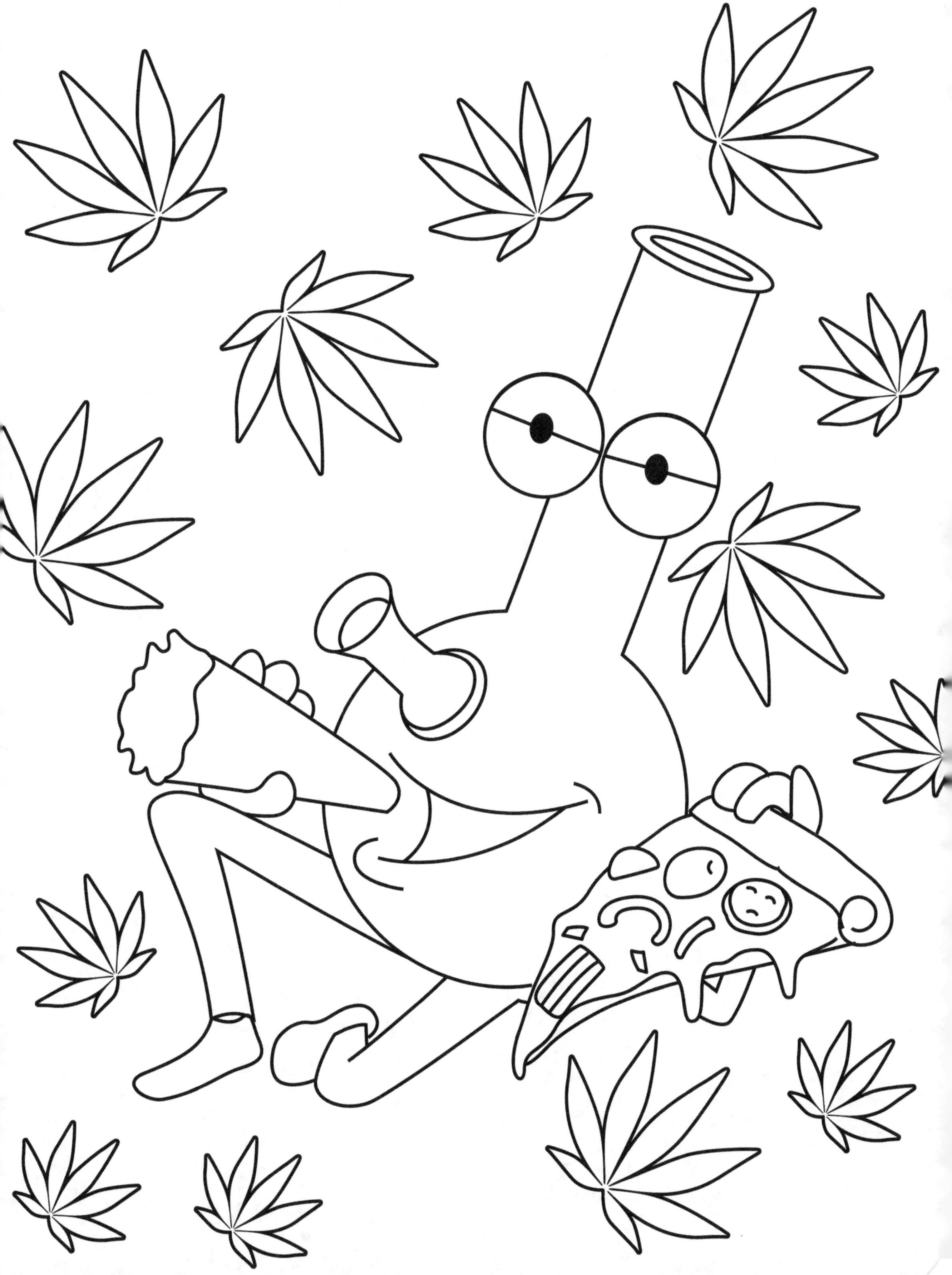

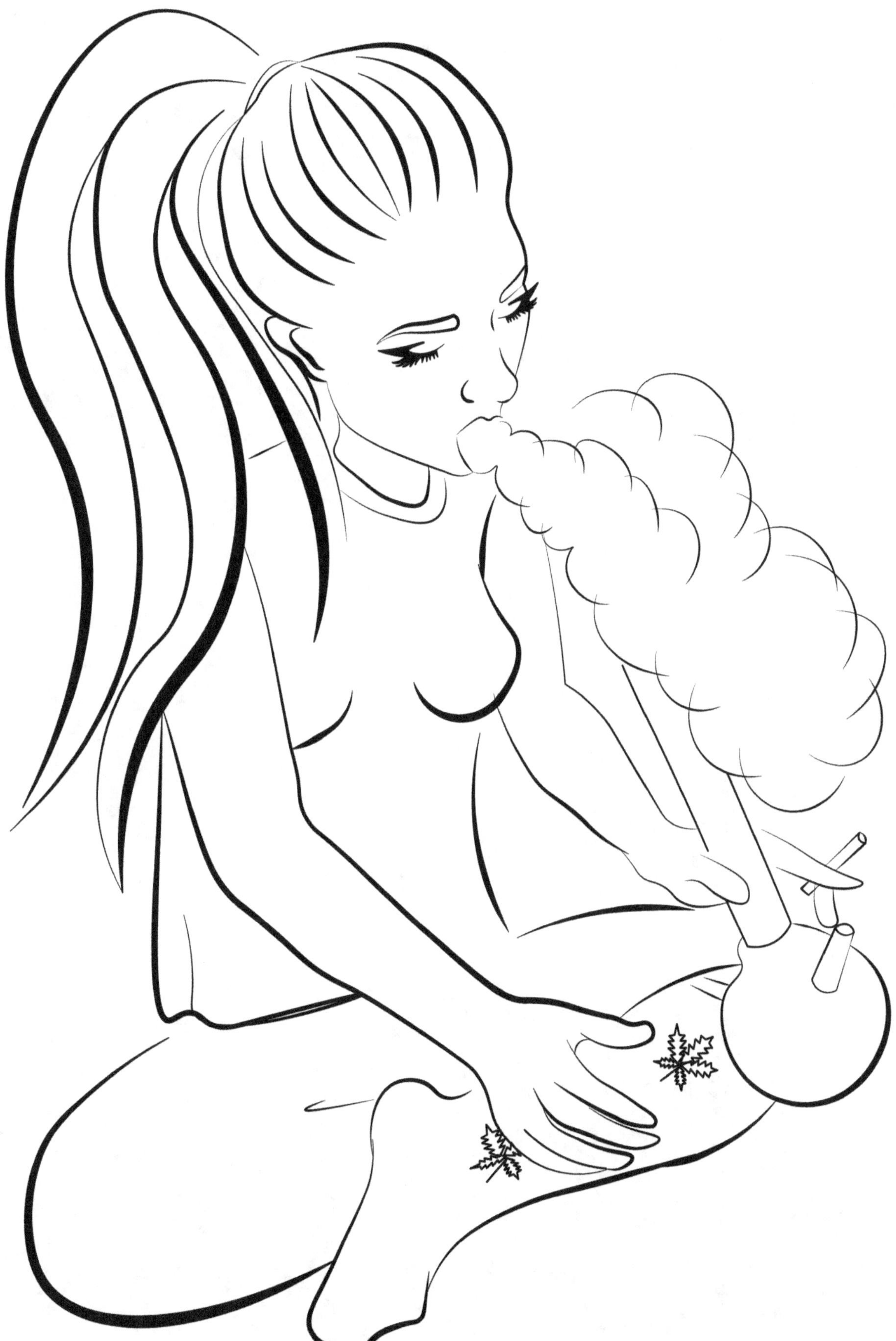

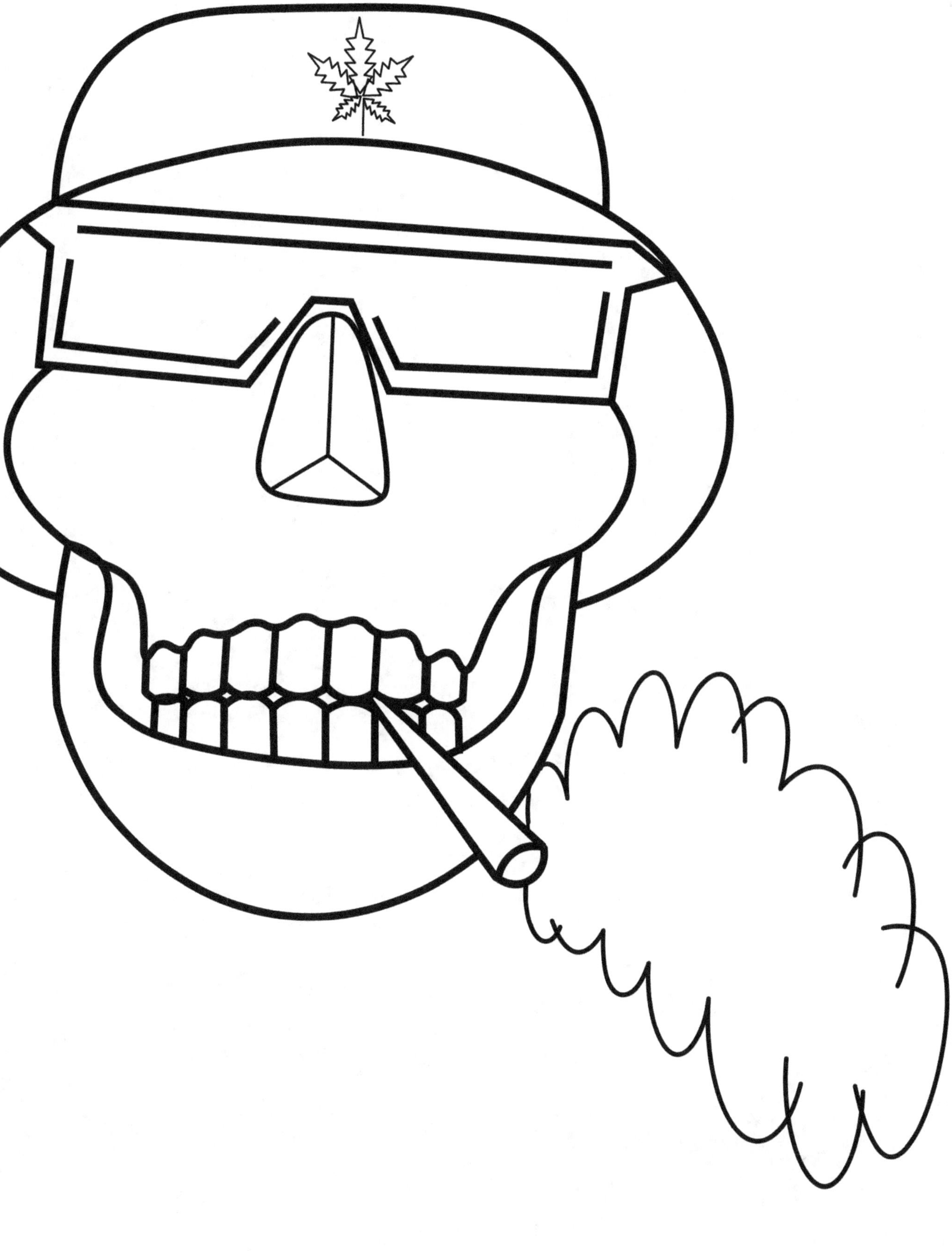

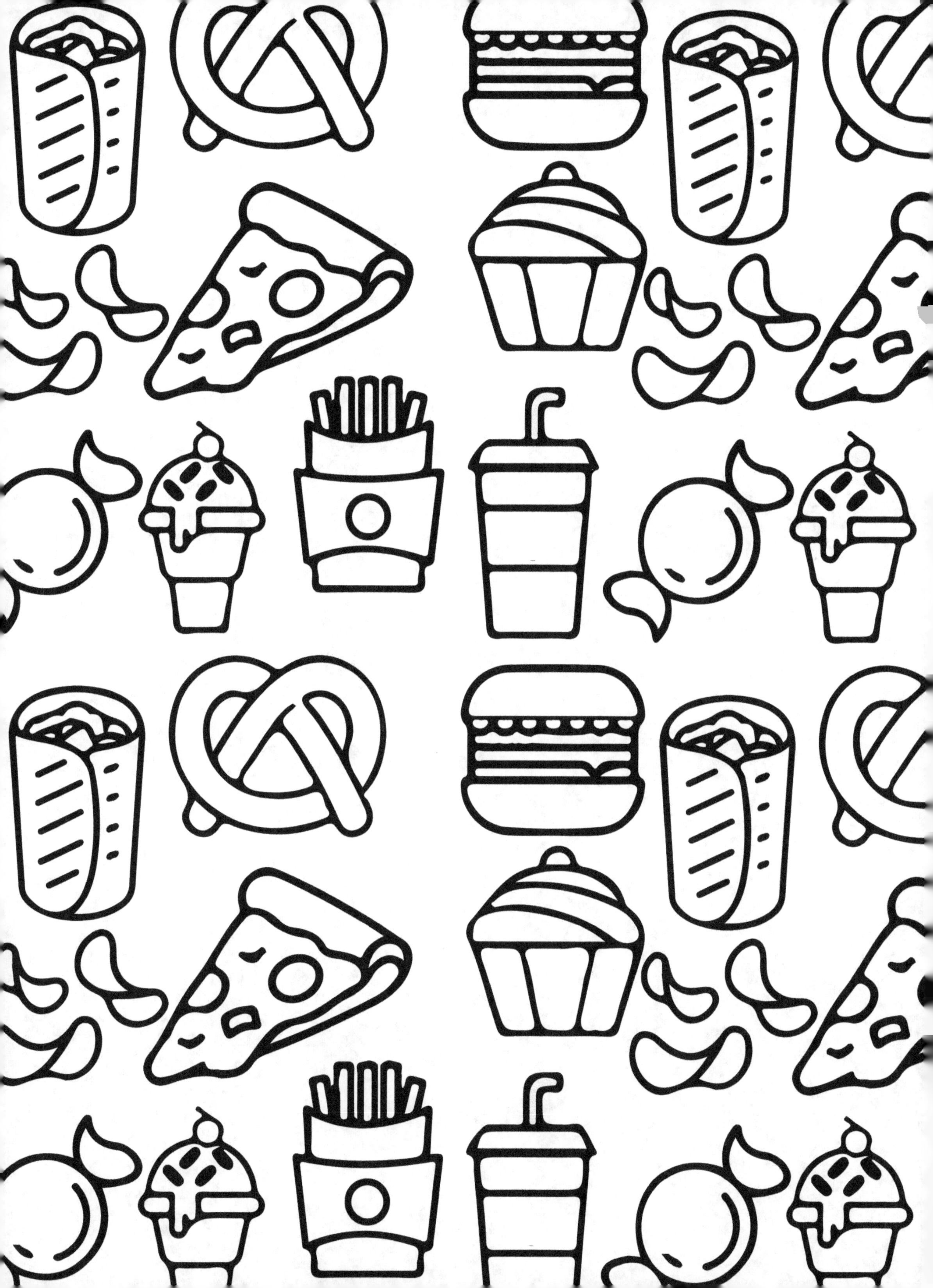

Color Test Page

More Fresh Baked Marijuana Coloring Fun!

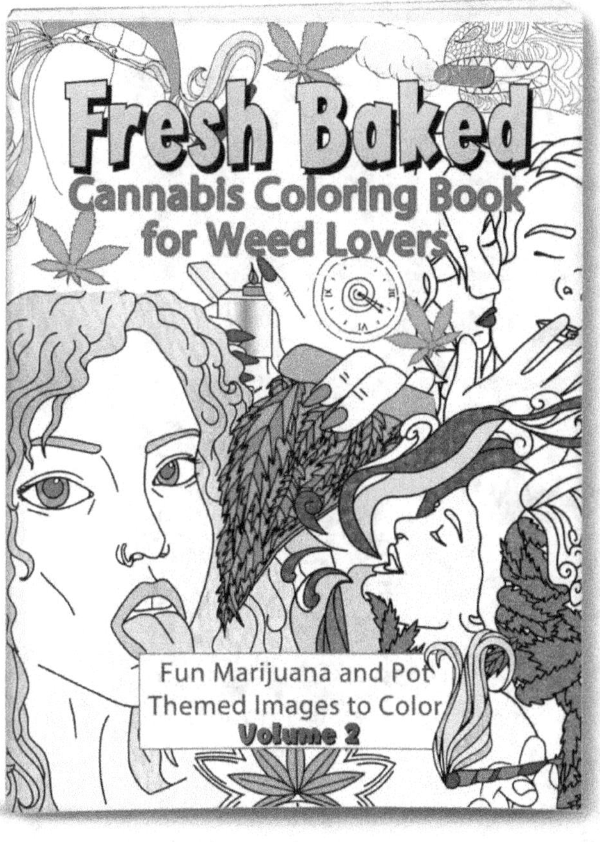

Amazon: 1947676148

ISBN: 978-1947676145

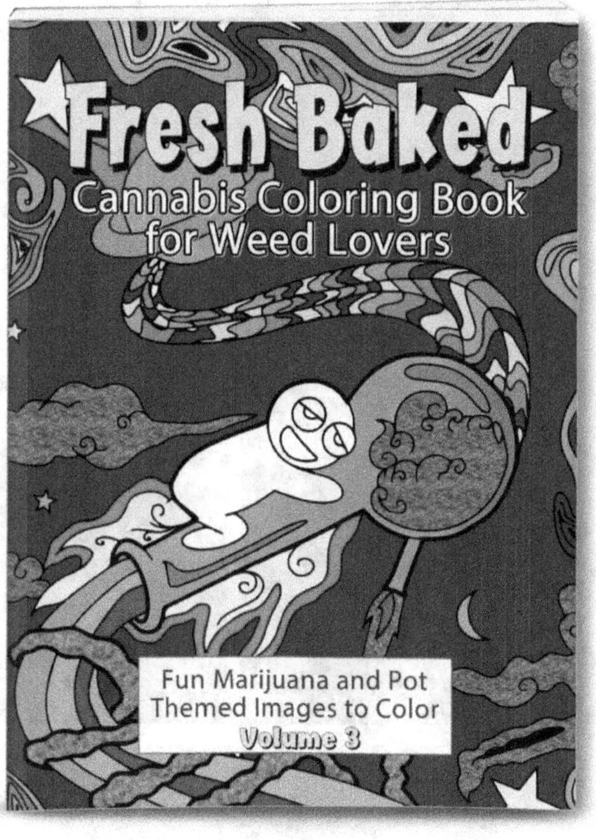

Amazon: 1947676156

ISBN: 978-1947676152

AMAZING Color Art.com

Enjoy these great titles and more by Amazing Color Art!

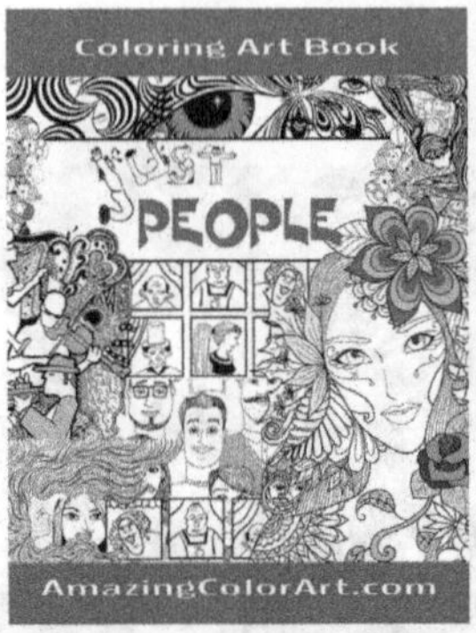

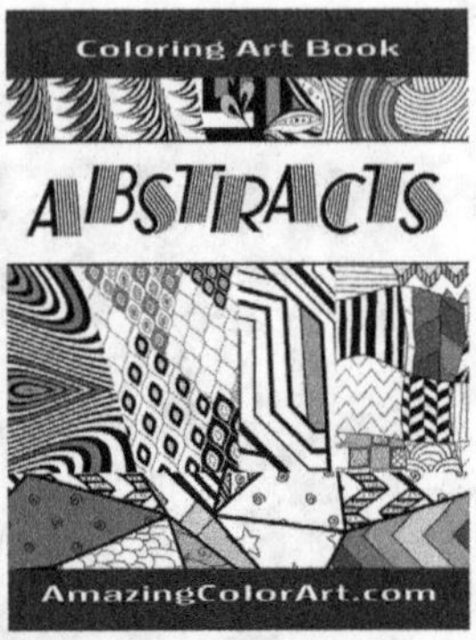

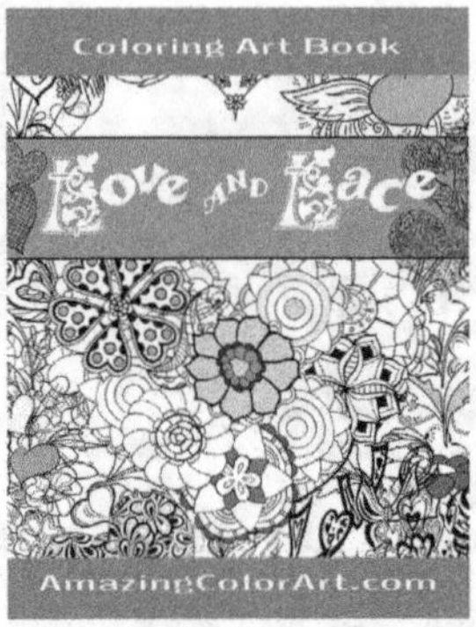

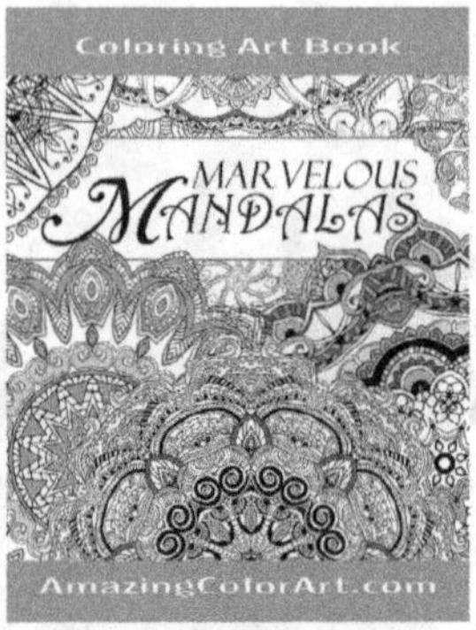

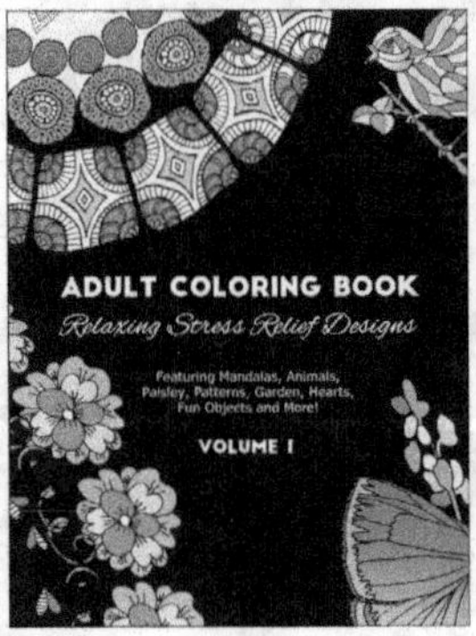

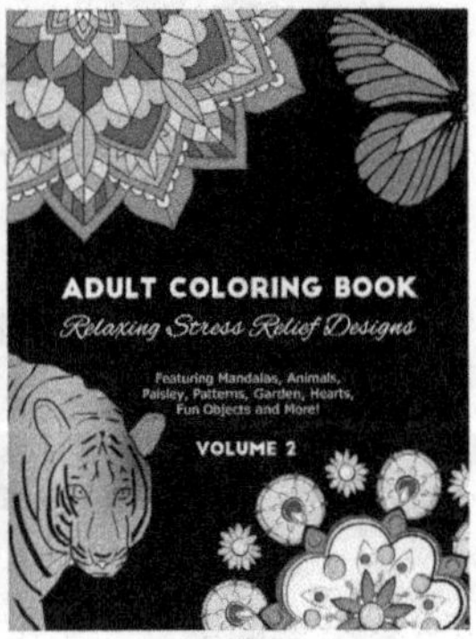

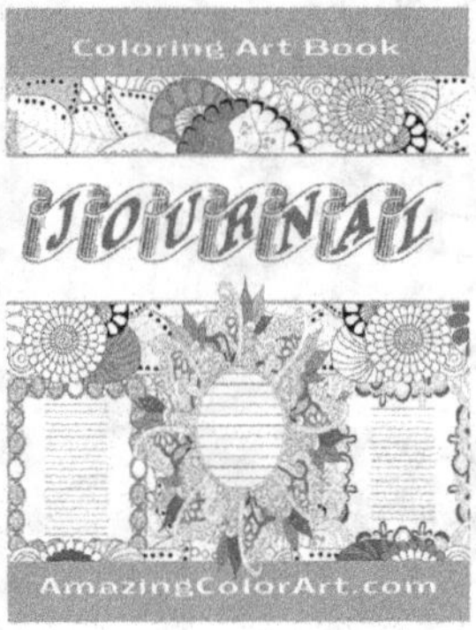

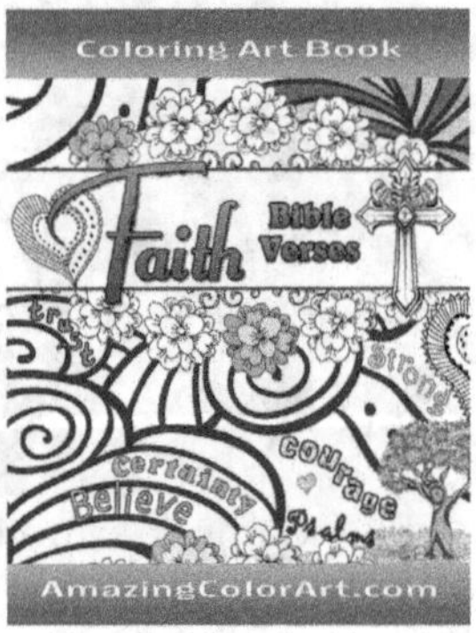

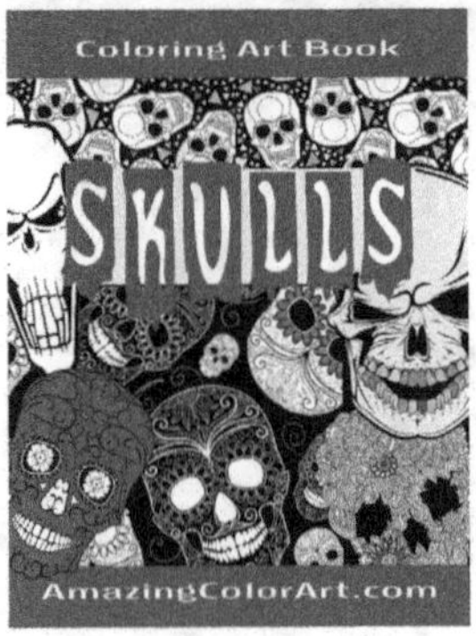

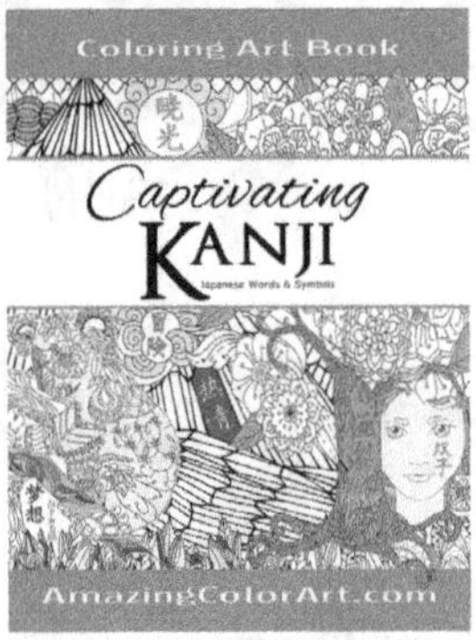

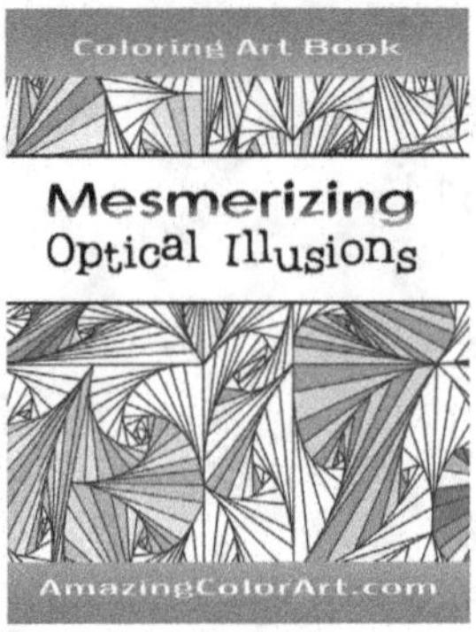

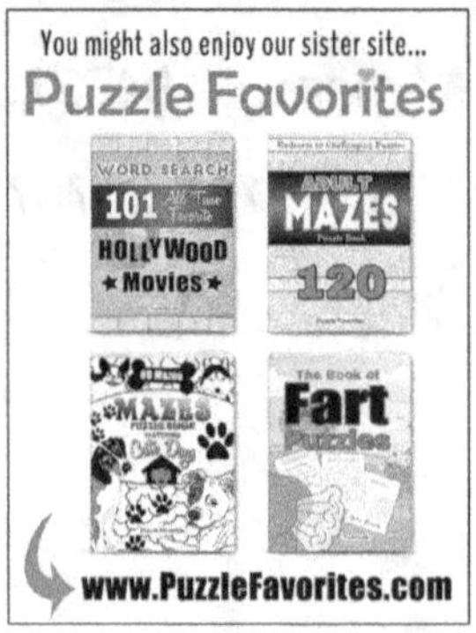

www.ingramcontent.com/pod-product-compliance
Lightning Source LLC
Chambersburg PA
CBHW081612220526
45468CB00010B/2851